A LEAP WITHIN

A LEAP WITHIN

Ameya Agrawal

KALPAZ

ISBN : 978-93-5128-121-4

Price : ₹ 250

First Published, 2015

Published by

Kalpaz Publications
C-30, Satyawati Nagar
Delhi-110052, Ph. : 9212142040
E-mail: kalpaz@hotmail.com

Printed at : G. Print Process, Delhi

Cataloging in Publication Data—DK
Courtesy: D.K. Agencies (P) Ltd. <docinfo@dkagencies.com>

Agrawal, Ameya, author.
A leap within / Ameya Agrawal.
pages cm
ISBN 9789351281214

1. Life. 2. Life skills. 3. Agrawal, Ameya. I. Title.

DDC 113.8 23

Contents

Dedication

This book is dedicated to my parents who developed me into '*Ameya*'

-Ameya Agrawal

PRAISES FOR THE BOOK

"The book seems truly engrossing. Ameya have an ability to connect to people in a simple yet profound manner with his writing. I am sure he will make it really big in life as the book will also."

-Dr.Radhakrishnan Pillai,
Best-Selling author of 'Corporate Chanakya'.

"The book is very promising. I like his (Ameya's) new style of language and vocabulary".

-Hon. C.M Bhandari,
Yog Guru,
Former Ambassador of India to Poland, Lithuania, UAE, Cambodia.

"The content is excellent, writing style very simple and points- easy to relate to. There are hundreds of Self Development books, which focus more on Development than the Self. His style of writing seems to focus more on the 'Self'. Wishing him most and more."

-Mr. Arun Davay,
Founder, Chief Consultant, Mind Matters.

"'A Leap Within', helps to explore many known but unfelt feelings. It's not just a self-help or motivation book but a complete package. I wish Ameya Agrawal 'The very best' and looking forward for many more such good books in the coming days."

-Prof.Bholanath Dutta,
Known as Management Samrat,
Visionary Edupreneuer
Founder, President & Convener of
MTC Global

"The Book is amazing and Ameya Agrawal has done a really great job. Keep it up and may God bless you."

-Mr. Shailajakant Misra,
Former IPS officer, popularly known as the "Supercop"

FOREWORD

While I was in my office doing my daily works, I received a call from Ameya. He told me about his upcoming book *'A Leap Within.* It was a pleasant surprise to know that a kid I met three years back during his AIEEE exam has achieved such a great height and has grown up so much that he has authored a book and not a novel but a self-help book. When he told me to take a look on his work, I was excited to know what a guy at young age of 19 can write and what he has to give the world. But when I read the book I realized that this generation is developing at a rate faster than our imagination.

The way he put up his views and the blend of various experiences and short stories wherever needed made this book interesting to read. One never gets bored of picking up any chapter from anywhere to read. You neither need to have a dictionary nor a very complex mind to understand what is written inside. The lucid writing and the keen and sharp observation made by him astonished me.

The way he explained many little points may it be professionalism or human habits or about love, everything touches the heart of the reader and inspires them in true sense. Quotes like *"Kitni bhi ho kamai, lagta hai ki vo kam aai"* and his personal observations made me sure that this guy is not just a 19 year teenager but also has an excellent potential to lead.

This book surely help you to get an edge over cut throat competition. I appeal everyone to read this book as it will surely touch your heart and will leave a mark on your life in a good way.

I wish very best luck to Ameya that he continue his good work by leading people to the correct direction and keep surprising us.

-Dr. Pawan Agrawal, Ph.D(Mumbai Dabbawalas)
International Motivational and Tedx Speaker.

FROM DR. SANJAY UPADHYE

As the world gets entangled more and more in the web of materialistic pursuits, there is a strong fear that 65% of India's population, which consists of youth, will also lose its way in it. To provide a silver lining to this dark cloud comes a young college student, who writes a book that takes a very serious view of life.

I congratulate Ameya Agrawal from the bottom of my heart for writing this path-breaking book! What do I mean by 'bottom of my heart? If one has to know this, one has to read this book *'A Leap Within'* by Ameya, in which **he has viewed life both from 'with-in' and 'with-out'**. In this book, he embarks on a remarkable journey in which his turbulent thoughts travel between his unformed mind and this vast universe, both from 'with-in' and 'with-out'.

I feel any journey makes a person happy and I am sure that experiencing the described in this book will also make all of you happy. A poem in Marathi describes common people are like insects who seek their goals outside. Here, **Ameya is turning inside to seek for his goals**. It is not that I agree with all of his opinions.

But *"Experience is a male companion of growing age and Imagination is a girlfriend of any age!"* All the best for his 'imagination'!

-Dr. Sanjay Upadhye

Executive Director of Vishwa Shanti Sangh, Pune.

(Dr. Sanjay Upadhye is a well-known orator and humorist popularly known as "Gappashtakkar" in Marathi world)

WORDS OF GRATITUDE

I am glad that at this young age life and my inner self made me explore so many things, my heart and brain absorb experiences and help me learn from them.

This life wouldn't have been possible without my parents who believed there is something special in me as well in the book and made me believe too. **My Papa (Dr.Ashok Agrawal) taught me that when I decide to trust my instincts, no goal is too far. My Mumma (Dr.Kalpana Agrawal)**, who like every mother in the world, understood her child, encouraged me and didn't let me sit a moment wasting time when it came to my holistic development. I even saw tears in her eyes and the way she looked at me realizing how I grew up since those years, when I still used to cry to eat by her hand. I dedicate my first creation to my creators, **'My Mom and Papa'**.

Since I was a school going kid my teachers and their guidance, kept on inspiring and motivating me that I am destined for something different and something beautiful. My school (Biyani School, Bhusawal), College (Nahata College, Bhusawal) and MIT College of Engineering played a very important role in my character building.

The real reward I received was on the eve of New Year when I was blessed by **Dr. Radhakrishnan Pillai** with his motivational message. It was his greatness that he appreciated the book. It boosted my confidence like anything and so my responsibilities. It was one of the happiest moments for me. I wish readers will also feel the same happiness while reading. I find no word to express my gratitude for the great personality.

It was also a privilege to receive blessings from Hon. **Mr. C.M Bhandari**, Yoga Guru, and India's Former Ambassador.

I am also thankful to Mr. ShailajakantMisra and Sudeep Nagarkar who appreciated the book and wished me for successful future.

I express my sincere gratitude to Prof. Dr. Vishwanath Karad, Founder of MIT Institutions for taking a look at my work and further boosting my self-confidence with blessings.

I am thankful for the blessings of Hon. Mr. Rahul Karad, Executive Director, MAAERs Group of Institutions who was as happy as me when he came to know about this book and supported me whole heartedly.

I am thankful to Dr.Sanjay Upadhye, Executive Director, World Peace Centre and Prof. Dr. R.V Pujeri, of MITCOE for their support.

I don't think this book would have been in your hand without the guidance and support of my mentor Prof. Dipali Chandak, Nashik who is also like an elder sister to me. I received everything from her- inspiration, guidance, motivation, support. She is making things possible for me since day one.

My brother – *My Bhau Seth* (CA. Ajay Agrawal) and my Bhabi (CA. Kavita Agrawal) are always there supporting me at the back and front end.

My love, my nephew Aryan, made a person like me realize that small kids aren't that hard.

The fun I had while writing this book with my friends, my roommates and my buddies will be always there in my heart.

My publisher, Kalpaz Books took every efforts to publish this book in a beautiful way. I am thankful to them.

I am thankful to everyone who in one or another way were attached in making this dream come true and made me realize that "When you pursue your dreams, the whole world conspires to make It happen"

And at last but not least, I would like to thank all those who were anxious regarding this book, and were constantly updating themselves regarding the release of this book. It is not just mine but their dream came true!

I welcome not only Suggestions but also criticism which will be helpful for continuous better creation.

'Let Us Take A Leap Within'

-Ameya Agrawal

You can reach Ameya Agrawal at
contact.ameya99@gmail.com
9158715200
Twitter- @ameyaagrawal
www.facebook.com/aleapwithin

PREFACE

I don't actually remember from where it started and how it did. But it just started somewhere deep inside me when I was just unknown of the world, counting values of 'x' in mathematics, studying about Shivaji Maharaja in history lessons. It started when I used to be busy in doing homework, running behind grades, it used to feel different because like I was just not that kid who was thinking about stealing the sweets from mom's safe and used to cry for chocolates in front of dad. There was always a thought in the mind that whatever I am or whomsoever I relate to, is the only significance to be here in, to grow old, do a job and die. Every act that used to happen related to me or not used to drop me somewhere in the middle of Deep Ocean of thoughts.

What inspired me to write this? Just wanted to do something different from all the mainstream stuffs, I used to jot down everything that used to inspire me, teach me and felt inside after watching around. But I always misplaced it so this time decided to be serious as I wanted to utilize my hobby into something professional and an inner wish to start something early to make my parents proud.

You must be wondering why another book on life? Actually, yes there you are! Why another book needed to learn life? Man! Life is not a subject or a part of academic curricular to go and learn, it's something to go out and just enjoy the way you like it.

We are already busy learning so many things we don't actually know where and why we will use them. Why are we learning them? So why add another burden to stack full of impending things to learn? Now here my professionalism comes in. Why to go for this book when so many great and renowned people already hoisted their flags with some great books in this field on HOW TO LIVE A *PERFECT* LIFE?

Excuse me!! What?? Perfect life??Are you sure?

> *"**Life is** not a slut to be **easy**, it's a bitch."*

What I learned is,

> *"First, we don't **respect** things that we get **easy** and later cry when **things** get complicated."*

Life is governed by 3 simple actions- Eat, Pray, Love.

What else one needs!

Perfect life is just a mirage and its better that it is. How can one enjoy if something is perfect? You will miss the different tastes if you just keep eating one of your favorite foods. This book will surely help to understand those little things in life which we all see but never actually experience. Those things which are always around us trying to teach us something inspiring us, but are never given the attention. It is not a 'Perfect Life'medication, but surely a well enjoyed one. This book will help you not to regret the small amounts you missed in the past. It will help you to see things through different perspectives. It can inspire you to come out of the old orthodox rule book and build your own game.

Actually, it's not a book with various researches done on human psychology or some high level words. It depicts just the common observations. Just prepare yourself to witness some of the most close, but unknown feelings, situations, moments and their significance.

This book actually doesn't concentrate on a single topic and keep grating it. It comprises of many little yet important lessons, big yet easy things that I observed and felt throughout these years.

It completely depends on how you take this book, how you feel and how you apply this in your life. The one thing I am sure about is, while reading this book and going through each and every line, every distinct word, you will see yourself somewhere. You will feel the complete environment as you experienced back and are going to experience in future. I can forecast the smile.

You must be wondering what different and worth reading this book contains? Actually you are right, no inspiring book contains new and the same is in this case, but it's not *any* inspiring book.

It's just depends on the way any author expresses it. I am not saying they mislead you, but instead of eating the food straight to your mouth these books make you eat around your head.

A one liner quote contains all the moral a 200pages book does. I may feel proud that I can write all these, but we might have not realized that again the Einstein's 'Theory of Relativity' works here.

For me it may feel good, but some may think I am just another psychological freak from engineering college as everyone tends to be after a span of time. It may feel proud that I think so much, but for those who just needs to live a life, it's a total waste of time.Feeling proud of what you like and what you do is good as people from ages told us. But for me, it's not that important unless you can inspire others to be like you. Because *it's just like smelling your shit and being happy about it because it's yours.* They say, do what you want and don't worry about people. It's kinda incomplete. Because, the life we lead is a place where the society plays an important role. If you are not loved by people you are just a freak who thinks the person in the mirror isthe only society.

But the people whose views and feelings towards us are important are those who make our life, who we love and who will be always there. Because *if we keep thinking about what everyone thinks, then what will remain for them to think*?

This concept strikes the love too. Your woman may not be the best in the world. But if she is the best for you, then you should be that person to her in front of whom she will never remember Ranbir Kapoor or Salman Khan.

Because if she still *thinks "If I happened to be luckier I could have got this or that person"*then your couple is not different from the heard of those animals in the jungle whose mere goal of life is eating and extend the tribe, while female just keep searching for the strongest male.

"Women keep searching for ***Superman*** *their whole life, but fail to realize that they were living with* ***Clark Kent*** *the whole time"*

Sometimes I feel why everything is so complex under the name of being civilized? Why one needs to understand someone else's mentality instead of handling his own? Why someone needs to study people's behavior? Why they need the books of excellence and books on how to do this or how to do that? How to succeed? How to become rich? How fool are we? We spend half of our life in learning how to earn money, then we waste another half in learning how to spend money. First, we have time to enjoy which we spend in running behind material world and when we achieve our greed we remain with no capacity to enjoy. As someone rightly said,

"During childhood we have energy and time but no money, then during early adulthood, we have energy and money but no time and when we grow older we have time and money but no energy."

We spend so much of time learning and predicting to be civilized that we are left with regret at the end that we did nothing in spite of having all those facilities. These laws, rules, restrictions, constitutions we say are making our life more proper simpler and healthier, but I wonder is there any life in this life. May be if this is not for the present condition of the world, I wouldn't have got an opportunity to write this book and express myself because even I would have been hanging to the trees, jumping here and there eating bananas, hooting across the jungle with leaves wrapped around my waist.

"I don't want to teach ***people*** *anything, I* ***just*** *want to make them* ***realize"***

THE BEGINNING

We all started our lives as a child, many things never leave us since then. Competitions, emotions and our attitude. Even when in the mother's womb, if you are with your sibling there is a competition of getting the highest nutrition and sustain your growth. This competition further carries on in our life in a bigger or smaller way, getting entrance to school, in sports and in love.

Competition can do only two things, either it teaches man the true attitude and gives him the vision to get to the top, inspires him with adventures throughout his life, makes him confident, teaches him to choose the right path or make the chosen path right or it can completely break the moral and morale of a person. It depends how we pursue it.

The world gets complicated with every new invention. It seems that the things have become so easy now as compared to that in the past, but if taken a proper look with a right thought we can easily realize that we are just making ourselves dependent on things under the name of comfort. Most of the things we are abiding ourselves to use today, things without which we cannot imagine our life are just making us more and more dependent. Instead of getting standing on our own legs, rising above the limitations, we are falling prey to them.

And here is how you can use this for your professionalism. Here again rises the competition. The competition to make public dependent on our product so that they will have no option but to make your company richer and richer. Companies take the benefit of the needs (artificially generated) of the customers, to fill their pockets. The general human psychology is very important in this scenario. Once you start showing people that they need something and it can make their life easier and comfortable and can make them look stand apart from the society, the customers transfer those things on their list from the want section to basic needs because *needs and wants are two different things.* Once you start considering the things you want as the things you need then there is no way out.

*"**Needs** should be given priorities and not the **wants.**"*

They are often disguised to us.

I remember the time when I was living with my roommates during the engineering years. My friends were from middle class family and I was certainly more privileged than them.

They all used to take out money from the ATM according to the need, like 500 bucks for the week and on the other hand I used to bring cash from home and was never bothered about the lack of money. There used to be times when they used to say "Dude, I don't have the money today, dad is yet to deposit the money in the account" and I used to feel happy"wow! I have money." But once cash with me got over and I was not able to go to the ATM for some reason and was left with some 200 rupees. That was the first time I said "Bro, I can't buy stuffs today, let's do it next time, don't have enough money" and trust me that time I didn't feel bad at all. It was kind of feeling free. No worries, no tension, no plans were there to check out and hence my mind was free that yes I got no stuffs to worry about.

The second incident was when my cell phone got broke down, till that time I was a phone addict. No single moment ever passed when I was not thinking that did I receive something? Is there any important message from someone? Did he/she replied? If yes, then what if no then why not? Even If I switch it off I used to worry that I should not miss some important stuff, I was suffering from FOMU- Feeling of Mobile Unattended, but when my cell phone got broke down, it untied my strings with Facebook, WhatsApp, internet and its addiction as well. I knew that my phone has stopped working and I can't do anything so my mind automatically stopped thinking about it and it got free from all the thought processes that use to boggle me when the phone was running. Though it has disconnected me, partly from the world, it made me feel free and so I can take out time for myself.

The reason to mention the above incidences is that, there are times when we are needed to cut our connection from the outer world and take out time for ourselves. Sometimes we should free ourselves from the luxuries and materialistic world and experience how it feels to be under the open sky without the ceiling.

We should learn that if there are some problems we cannot do anything about then why to worry about it, leave it to God and check yourself out how open and relaxing it feels. Sometimes instead of worrying about my phone, my heart decided to accept the fact and adapted to the situation and at that time I was feeling more relaxed than I used to feel before.

"If the ***problem has a solution*** *then why to worry about it and if it don't, then what's the use of worrying"*

Stephen Hawking, one of the greatest physicists ever, is reported to have said that we live on a minor planet of a very average star located within the outer limits of one of a hundred thousand million galaxies. How's that for a shift in perspective? Given this information, are your troubles really that big? Are the problems you have experienced or the challenges you might currently be facing really as serious as you have made them out to be?

"Don't let your ***Education*** *ruin your* ***knowledge"***

Education and knowledge without common sense has little meaning. Common sense is the ability to see things as they are and do them as they ought to be done. We are born with five senses- Touch, Taste, Sight, Smell, and Hearing. But successful people have the sixth sense- Common Sense. Common Sense is gained in spite of, not necessarily as a result of education. The best education without common sense is worthless. *An abundance of common sense is called Wisdom.*Sometimes too much of education is not only harmful, but can make us look a fool in our own view once we realize it.

Nowadays everyone has become very intelligent and smart to understand that this education system we are learning through, especially here in India is not going to help the way through and is not right.

Here we concentrate on what we can show and not on what we know, but that's not completely wrong either.You get a price for what you see. While on the other hand the system is not completely correct is what I feel while being in the trend of engineering.

Though I am pursuing my degree in *Electronics and Telecommunication* stream, if you will come and ask me tomorrow what the basics of transistor and how it works, I will have to think for a couple of minutes. I may be able to solve all those complex numericals and circuits given in the reference books throughout these four years of my engineering student life, but I still don't know where I am going to use it. You must have thought "Go and ask your teacher,man!!." Is it that easy? Where everyone is busy solving and understanding those circuits, it's awkward to go and ask teacher "Ma'am, why are we studying these circuits?" Am sure after four years more than 80% people will forget what the hell we solved back then.

Indeed a field of interest is necessary to be chosen when you are selecting your career. Education we take should also inspire us to go out of the rule book, stand tall and show the world our caliber.

"In India, the day people will start using their learner's instincts instead of the survival instincts in the **education**, *our society will no longer be a place where education kills our* **knowledge**.*"*

It should not feel that you are sitting in a classroom learning something which you are going to go and apply in some or other company. Why are we taught that do this do that? Be like this, be like that because this company wants this or this company wants that during the placement. Why we are taught to just work for one or another company? Why are we taught to be workers and not leaders? I firmly believe that,

"One's goal **in life** *should* **be** *getting* **inspired** *about what they can do with passion* **and not** *to*

wake up with **regret** *everyday to curse the system that forces them in this situation"*

I may feel diplomatic in what I said. Because if you take a lookwhile being in class I realized that all this seriously affect our lifestyle.Like two fingers are not same, it is not necessary that two people will think in the same direction.

Some people just want to learn, earn, raise a family and die. Some people feel like this life is just a mask. And they start finding the truth. Some people don't understand what the hell this is till last and the remaining people are those few guys who know all these things IN and OUT of life and decides to take what it throws at them with a powerful hit back shot and achieve high and touch the sky.

Basically, these are those people who believe that the world is how we see it and no doubt in this that these people go forward and fill our history books with lots of stuffs to remember, learn and understand. Truly said that

"Beauty lies in the eyes of beholder."

For those people who belong to this category the classroom feels like an institute of slave training. A training after which the institutes are going to put you In front of your masters-companies and they will choose the person they want.

I wonder whether companies want well informed, well educated people with critical thinking. This may be against their interests. They want obedient workers, people who are smart enough to learn the paperwork and run the machines, intelligent enough to bring something innovative and dumb enough to take pride in it, raise the company to heights and passively accept it

Seeing through the eyes of such people it feels like life is not just a show or something in which you have to act only because you came into it.

I once heard during my college days that some companies are developing such technology where suppose you are working for that company, you are at your desk, sitting in front of your desktop and you don't touch the keyboard for a specified time then a message goes to your boss that you are not working and consequences you know. Your boss is going to call you, scold you, shout at you. "Why you are not working, are you paid for doing this shit?" So here now if I am not wrong doesn't that feels like the Hollywood or Bollywood movies where they buy the slaves and hire them for work and suppose you don't work the masters swing their hunter and whip you.

*"**You** know you **are** on the right path if you are doing **yourjob** and not be paid for it"*

-Oprah Winfrey

I also learned that Microsoft or some companies have busses fully equipped like the office, computers, desks and everything else like internet facility. Now a normal man will think about it like 'Wow!! How advanced their systems are, how much progress they had made" but the real thing behind it is that, the companies want you to serve them even when you are riding from home to your job, they don't want a single minute of yours to go waste because it causes wastage of thousands of minutes for them collectively.

I don't think that will sound good if you think about the real part behind it.

I agree the companies give a handsome salary and bonus in cash and kind, they provide you with an iPhone, a laptop, bungalows, car, but ever thought that how much of us get these, it's for sure about the quality, it's for sure given to those only who deserve it, they are right that they can't give it to any random person, you need to have that caliber.

And when I told this same to my parents, they said why don't I try to be that one person who is bestowed with all those gifts, why don't I work harder and earn it, I was like "Work *harder??!!", I know I should but that's what the companies want, they show us the greed of appraisals and took out the work from us but excuse me for a second, here again, I don't mean that to prevent the company from making a profit we should stop working or stop developing ourselves.*

Rise for ourselves, stand for ourselves, fight for ourselves, and create for ourselves, won't that will be much better to be the creator of our own destiny, source of income, and not only us but the creator of job for thousand others. That would be far better and well accepted I guess. And no one can deny this one fact that the happiness you get after building your own fort with your own hands have some unmatched kind of feeling, isn't it?

The problem is that

> *"Contrary to foreign countries where students are working on innovative ideas, and are reinventing the technology, meanwhile in India we feel proud to be a worker in their mega projects striving to make their dreams come true while simultaneously chocking those of India"*

But wait a second, I hope the route is not going the wrong way and I hope I am not misleading you. I'm not discouraging you to do a job. I'm neither against those who prefer jobs, nor do I feel that they have a low reputation. Because at the end of the day, it's all about perspective, and the way you follow it.

> *"Kuch log* **mangal** *(Mars) par jeevan dhund kar khus he, to kuch log jeevan me* **mangal** *dhund kar"*

Some want a peaceful, secured life where the *wants* and *needs* are not much where they have to just earn enough to let the two ends meet with some space and expenses for fun stuff and chilling out and fulfil their fond. They want a calm life where there is no risk a constant approach a constant payment, time for family, time for self, just enjoy and be happy with what they have, and there is nothing wrong in this, nothing at all. That's another cool way of living, we should try someday too.

But for some just this much is not enough, just working for earning money so that you can spend it to fulfil some of your needs or wants is not only they want. They also want time for themselves, time for family, but they just don't want this much only. They want a little more, they want it big. As the Royal Stag advertisement says "Have I made it large". For them the sky is the limit is small word, because their word limit fails to exist.

They like a life on a roller coaster. Stopping doesn't appear in their dictionary and loosing is what they never heard of. Adjusting themselves, even when they can do better to what they have is never possible for them,

I remember once I was travelling from Nashik to Pune. Behind me some lady was sitting, she was probably talking to her son who tends to appear for some interview in IT sector. Her conversation was clearly understood. She was telling her son that the company he was opting for is one of the best companies in the world, she advised him to dress properly, wear good shoes and not slippers, properly comb hair so that his impression should be good on the company, she further told him to answer them properly whatever question they ask, and when they finish asking questions and ask him whether he have any questions for them, she told him to ask various questions like "What will be the working hours? What will they pay him?", she addressed that, "don't worry, the company is good, you will get holidays, five days a week you have to work, you are in better company than your cousins."

Whatever she was teaching and guiding him must be the manners or code of conducts and I agree you need to follow those because that is the way the world works on the wheels of systematic behavior and proper protocols which you are needed to be followed.

But at such situation, I don't know what my ego or my self-respect tingles me and I feel like it won't be better if instead of sitting in front of those authorities, we are the authority and people are preparing so much to meet us, now someone will say "To reach that position you need to work as a worker, you need to follow them to learn, you must give respect to take respect. Yeah, exactly. They are right. "But though "To be a good leader you must be a good follower," but also "All Good followers don't make good leaders" you must not forget.

It may be my point of view, but the conversation felt very disappointing to me, it was feeling like his mom, she's putting up her son in some kind of marketplace, where the buyers will ask various questions, choose the worker they like, decide the working hours for how much time her son should serve that company. Assuring her son that his masters are much better than those where his cousins are working for. Being a labor or worker is not bad, it's not wrong. But never feeling to take a step forward, lead or develop yourself is a crime. A crime you commit to yourself.

"Boss may be one, but a leader can be anyone"

What I think about this particular incident is that, it is our mentality that is forcing us to serve others as slaves. Especially in developing countries like India and the subcontinent. We should be encouraging the motto of creating jobs.

Whoever you see, wherever you see they just tell you to get placed somewhere in some company, whether big or small, even if you are genuinely intelligent they offer a bigger price to buy you, maybe 50lakhs or 20 million a year. But the background remains same- Work for someone else. Be a servant.

People should at least enhance their mindset by saying that "Work for a company for a particular span of time, learn from there how everything works and start something of yours". We are just sending our manpower to someone else, we are selling our excellence to West and then buying the products made by our men for a cost far greater and then again we hire employees to work and maintain these products and thus the cycle continues. We just offer the maintenance job to our people. *"Dude! At least take some care of dignity"*. This should definitely change else the day won't be far when we will have neither recognition, nor status of our own, but we will be looked upon as a nation which just serves the foreign land. We will be called as Slave, the IT slaves.

When I wrote that don't work for someone else, be your own boss, some may even think *"Be a master first then make people your slave"*

No!! It doesn't mean that. There are people who want a stable life, who are willing to extend services in exchange of currency and such people are best for jobs. There is a difference between doing a job because you find it interesting and taking up a job because there are no other options for survival. Even being an entrepreneur is a job. Job must be of dignity, if you are satisfied with it, then do it. No one is capable of judging your capabilities on basis of 10 lakhs or 20 lakhs package. My mentor once told me,

"If ***everyone*** *will become entrepreneur then who will* ***work****"*

It is a like a chain, everyone has their assigned responsibilities and duties, the need is that to identify them and make best out of them. Always remember that

"You are never going to be remembered for the rules you follow, but for the rules you break"

And here by breaking rules I don't mean breaking the traffic signal, hacking into the World Wide Web, doing some sort of scam, bribing and whatever included in those stinky stuffs.

By breaking the rules, I mean breaking the old beliefs that ties our legs hard and mind stiff and don't allow us to think and proceed ahead. By breaking rules I mean kicking on the face of those who think that the only rule remained for success in the present time is the path of the wrong. The power, if righteous will always lead.

By breaking the rules, I meanthat even if you break the code of conducts, do it so efficiently and confidently that it will bring only the right consequences and for the right causes. Those hard guys who trust themselves and who know what's right, they break the rules, do their job and ensure their name with golden words in the great book of history. History honors them as legends, as heroes.

Let's consider a situation where right now there is a kid finishing parents' evening in a heated discussion with his mother, saying"Why does I have to study subjects which I am never supposed to use in my entire life?" And she would look at him blanked eyed, stifle a sigh, think for a second and then lie. She will say something along the lines of 'You know to get a good job you need to get a good degree, and these subjects will help you to get a good degree' she will say "You *are so lucky, you got all these facilities, we never had this opportunity when I was younger* "And he will reply "*But you were younger a long time ago, the time has now changed*".

And now she won't respond, knowing that whatever he is saying makes a sense, that societies' need would have changed since the time when his mother was younger of his age.

But still she will ignore him, grip his hand more sternly and drag him to thecar. Now at that moment what she doesn't know is that she didn't ignore him just to shut him up. She didn't lie because they are just returning from parents' evening and an argument in the hallway would look bad on her resume, she won't lie because she spends the last one hour convincing the stern face teacher that she would ensure her child study more at home. NO!! She lied because she doesn't know any better herself, although her whole adult life, she has never used the Pythagorean Theorem, nor the Einstein's equations, and she never needed to bother about if there were no gravity. She will rely on the society.

She will be happy and will feel proud when the society tells her that her child is so smart, the sharpest mind in the school and she has not to worry about anything as his future is bright and he is always going to get good grades. But does she know that her child is hyperactive, unfocused and easily distracted?

Friends, you and me we both know, but will fail to count the number of subjects we memorize just before the exam which won't be used in life ever.

Did anyone remember the number of 'A' grades we all strove hard day and night for, which won't be ever asked when you apply for a job? How many of us remember something just five minutes after the teacher says stop writing?

Suppose one month later after your results you realize that you missed the 1st rank by one mark, does that mean, remembering that one minute sentence would have made you a better person and well qualified for the job?

Don't we all have different abilities, thought process, experiences and genes? So how can we let people judge us and decide our future who don't know a bit about us?

But if it's correct do you mean Steve Jobs, Bill Gates, Edison, Einstein don't worth to be in society because they were never good at school or colleges. Exams are indeed the way of society telling what you worth but don't let them decide what you are. Edison once said

"Tomorrow is my ***exam****, but I am not afraid,*
because a single sheet of paper ***can't decide my***
future*"*

I don't mean don't care about exams, or just put them away, don't push them apart from you, I mean just don't let them decide what you are, don't let them control you and degrade your confidence.

First people decide and take up some idea then more than 75% people always think that they chose something wrong, something that is not their cup of tea. Almost all of them want to leave it and there I learned something. Instead of leaving what you have undertaken, why not complete it when you already came so far? Why not take out something cool from it?

Don't think I am talking double minded, or that I'm confusing you.

You can enjoy what you have chosen to. Life is not short. Once you learn to enjoy the situation you can bang up upon the world to set wave scattering all over.

Simply enjoying it is necessary. Why make it so complicated?

"They say hardwork beats talent when talent
doesn't work hard "

But if that is true and success is inevitable result of hard work, then every woman in Africa would be a millionaire.

"Destiny is a great excuse for failure"

"All that is gold does not glitter, not all those who
wander are lost;

The old that is strong does not wither, Deep roots
are not reached by the frost. From the ashes a fire
shall be woken, a light from the shadows shall spring;

Renewed shall be blade that was broken, the crownless again shall be king.

ABOUT LIFE

One is never angry about life, but just a bit confused, confused by the silent questions life posts in your notebook which you were never intended to open, the notebook which no one ever thought about. People are confused that one has to pass through such a roller coaster of emotions during his life, no one ever thought that you will have to pay every time you smile. Some people are so stressed about life that even when they smile it feels like they have to pay rent for it. But people fail to understand that one can get the pleasure of shade only in the sunlight.But if today your eyes are wet, let them flow, because trust me later if you even want to cry life mould you so hard and so stubborn that you can't even if you want to.

"When you grow up, you are tend to be told by people that the world is the way it is, your life is just a small part of it, live your life as it is in the world, try not to bash on the walls too much. That's a fear of limited life. Life can be much broader, once you discover one simple fact and that is that everything around you that you call life is made by people who are no smarter than you and you can change it, you can influence it, build your own things that others can use. Just shake off this erroneous (mistaken/flawed) notion that the life is there and you are just going to leave it forces it and embrace it. Change it, improve it, prove it and make your mark upon it and once you learn that you will never be the same again"-Steve jobs

Sometime in life, all we need is a little time,

to sit back, relax and compose a rhyme.

We need a time when we can sit by the window, look at the moon and count the stars,

we need a time when we can fill the happiness in our empty jars.

We need a time when we won't fill the books of sin, we need a time when we fill the emptiness that lies within.

We need a time when we can simply listen and we can simply sing,

we need a time when with the breeze we swing.

We need a time when we read books late night,

we need a time when with the world we unite.

We need a time when we play not to win,

we need a time when we play just to grin.

We need a time when we can fall asleep gazing at the distance far,

we need a time when we are not afraid of the scar.

We need a time when we can wake up with the rising sun,

we need a time when we have no need to run.

We need a time when our life is not governed by the world or the money we earn,

we need a time when if we turn

we have nothing to spurn.

We need a time when we are not leased not with the clocks or the tie,

we all just need a time that money can't simply buy.

Because all we need is to be boundless and free,

since we are the roots of the same tree.

We live in the society where the people are more concerned about the health of Amitabh Bacchan, the career of ShahRukh Khan and the *runs* Sachin Tendulkar makes rather than the health of the society career of self and the development Indians are lagging behind. We are happy because ShahRukh Khan is so rich and is earning twice in a day and four times in the night. We are happy because they are successful in their fields.

We are concerned about the likes these people have on Facebook or the box office collection they make. We are concerned to blame film industry why the film is rated as per money collection, but we fail to understand that it is us who get them that collection. We feel proud to call ourselves their fans and engage our self in competition to be the biggest one, but we never ever take one step forward so that tomorrow when you wake up on your birthday you need to be surrounded by security because millions of people are gathered in front of your house to wish you.

We use the internet at the speed of 50kbs and are in heaven when the speed gets to 120kbs for a moment, we are amazed and are satisfied just to see the speed of 10mbs in foreign countries, but we don't plan to work for ourselves to reach that level, because when we are upset with the speed we just Google, check what foreign countries has and are happy that "Wow!! How advanced the technology has got!"

By the simple example I just want to elaborate that we should not be satisfied with what we are juggling through the years. We must take a step forward initiate and excel.

There are 4 steps a human is tangled in

1) Being happy with whatever he has.
2) Window shopping.
3) Criticizing about what he doesn't like.
4) Really doing something about what he feels can be done better.

Only few people reach the 3rd step and these are those people you see on TV, read in the newspaper, wish to live a life like or you work for in your companies.

Once I came across a beautiful story which goes like this

A boat is docked in a tiny Mexican fishing village. A tourist complimented the local fishermen on the quality of their fish and asked how long it took to catch them.

"Not very long." They answered in unison.

"Why didn't you stay out longer and catch more?"

The fishermen explained that their small catches were sufficient to meet their needs and those of their families.

"But what do you do with the rest of your time?"

"We sleep late, fish a little, play with our children, and take siestas with our wives. In the evenings, we go into the village to see our friends, have a few drinks, play the guitar, and sing a few songs. We have a full life." The tourist interrupted,

"I have an MBA from Harvard and I can help you! You should start by fishing longer everyday. You can then sell the extra fish you catch. With the extra revenue, you can buy a bigger boat."

"And after that?"

"With the extra money the larger boat will bring, you can buy a second one and a third one and so on until you have an entire fleet of trawlers.

Instead of selling your fish to a middle man, you can then negotiate directly with the processing plants and maybe even open your own plant. You can then leave this little village and move to Mexico City, Los Angeles, or even New York City!

From there you can direct your huge new enterprise."

"How long would that take?"

"Twenty, perhaps twenty-five years." replied the tourist. "And after that?"

"Afterwards?

Well, my friend, that's when it gets really interesting, "answered the tourist, laughing. "When your business gets really big, you can start buying and selling stocks and make millions!"

"Millions? Really? And after that?" Asked the fishermen. "After that you'll be able to retire, live in a tiny village near the

Coast, sleep late, play with your children, catch a few fish, take a siesta with your wife and spend your evenings drinking and enjoying with your friends."

"With all due respect, sir, but that's exactly what we are doing now. So what's the point wasting twenty-five years?" Asked the Mexican.

And the moral of this story is:

Know where you're going in life, you may already be there! Many times in life, money is not everything. "Live your life before life becomes lifeless".

Being Rich doesn't always mean being happy. But still make sure you make a lot of it before talking such nonsense.

*"**Worried** about the boggling past*

*Tensed, about the **future** one can't cast.*

***Sad** about the pain,*

*Tied yourself to the endless **chain.***

***Frightened, we** are if the past don't change,*

*Worried about the **facts**, out of range.*

***Be** a soul, not a body*

*Leave everything else but the **toddy***

***Unleash** yourself from the past*

*Unleash yourself from the **future**,*

What's the use?

*Where, mere **being** un**happy** is the danger?"*

*"When you will **look back** you won't regret the lectures you bunked or any less percentage you scored, but surely those special moments you rejected **to** spend with your **loved ones**"*

"Only some people ***enjoy rain,*** *others just getwet"*

-Bob Marley

Have you ever fallen for someone and ***decide****d to do anything in the world* ***for*** *them cross your limits and make the most of it, if yes, make that someone* ***yourself*** *and do whatever shit you want to do!!*

-SUITS (Television Series)

The way of expressing the same can differ from person to person and age to age, but it all points towards the same direction.

If you look at relationships, love and everything related to it. You will find out that first people use to be proud of how nicely they can maintain a relationship or how truly they love someone and dedicated and happy they are about it.

And now if you go and ask someone you won't believe, but now people are finding proud of how nicely they can fool people and how good they are at taking out their work from others. They are now proud about how efficiently they can keep someone in disguise.

We are the creator of that world where it is more important for us to study if there exists a life on Mars and how they live, but we are not concerned if there is still life in us.

Like I mentioned earlier also, it can be put in different way also "*Humne mangal pe jeevan dhund ne ki jagah jeevan me Mangal dhundna chahiye*"

Which means that instead of finding life on mangal (Mars in English here) we should find mangal (peace and pleasance) in life.

"To ***live*** *is the greatest achievement in* ***the world*** *because others just exists"*

-Oscar Wilde.

Life blesses us with what we want. so we should better know and be careful about what we want and how much we want.

Life is full of truths surprises and experiments! During the journey of life we encounter several phases of life in the form of depression, success, happiness, loneliness, sadness, achievements and failure.When life teaches you, it teaches you hard, the lessons that are never forgotten and are never needed to learn again.

We are not always complaining about life, sometimes we are left wondering the methods and tricks life uses to show us around, we are left astonished by the views life wants us to see and the moments life wants us to live.

You can't just predict it and if you can, it is worthless. There may be some moments when laughing and giggling around you think that this is what life is, this is how the smile and happiness should be, but sometimes when you are smiling and enjoying around, you realize that the curve, the most beautiful curve of your lips is just for rent. The most important aspect of life is to learn from these. But do we do that, NO often not.

Above all the more devastating truth of life is the failure of ourself to accept them.We all know that failure and success are the two sides of the same coin called life, but we still fail to accept it, we know we have to die, but we never embrace death wholeheartedly, we all try to dodge it, we all want to go to heaven but none of us wants to die. Isn't that funny?

There are some inevitable truths we all have to live with

- ***The failure is on the cards:***

You cannot ditch failure, no one can. It is written on your cards already, you cannot change it. No one has tasted the success much sweeter without embracing the failure.

*"Whenever **life** hits you hard and goes away, wait a second, look back, **smile** a bit, look straight in her eyes and say ' Watch me'!"*

The Mother Nature teaches us the same. Grow rigorously each time you are cut down. The more they cut you, the more you should grow. Ever noticed when you cut down a tree with an axe to prevent its growth, the tree starts growing more rapidly and in a wild way. Or while you use razors to shave your beard or scissors to cut your hair, our hair starts to grow more quickly and also they become rough and harder.

This is how we are supposed to be, when we are put down, we should adapt and act more strongly towards it.

"**Go ahead,** fall down, the world looks different from the ground"

- Oprah Winfrey

- ***Success is not eternal:***

Accept it that it cannot stay with you every time, its dynamic and ever moving. Today it's yours and tomorrow it will be someone else's. Don't let it go, but when it does you need to be strong and accept it. Don't worry, it will come back again. It changes itsmaster frequently, probably the most unreliable friend of yours.

- ***Friends are not always trustworthy:***

Trust them, but not blindly.

- ***There is no escape to problems:***

Life is a struggle, it doesn't matter where you are brought up in favorable condition or unfavorable condition, and there is not escape to struggle. The greatest people braved to be the toughest resistance and struggle in their life. It is as true as death and life.

- ***Worries are destined:***

Worries and depression are inseparable part of our life. You me everyone has to encounter and face this stage of life sometimes now sometimes then but for sure. Without depression and worries the pleasure of happiness loses is ecstasy (Joy/ delight).

Without the bad times we don't understand the importance of the good time. Though we don't accept and welcome it, but we cannot avoid its existence.

If we could understand its worth we could understand life.

*"Why to worry about life so seriously, no one gets out **alive** in **any way**"*

- ***Destiny is not chosen:***

Quick success brings steep fall. Shortcuts to success are really the shortcuts but to failure. They can cut you short.No one else is responsible for your failure. It is only us who can control the cycle of our success and failure. Many people may come, help, support, stand and go, but to endeavor is your portfolio.

- ***Success is lonely:***

When you are standing at the hill top you have to stand alone. Because those who cares for you thinks that you are self-sufficient and will never ask whether you need their help or not and the other type is the type of jealous people who can never be yours, especially while you are standing at the top, You have to walk the road alone through the crowd of followers and admirers.

- **Needs are very little and wants are much higher:**

We have enlarged it by our burning desires. The basic needs are food, cloth and shelter, which are yet not accessible to millions. Others are just fake *wants* disguised as needs.

- ***Envy is your biggest enemy:***

When we keep grudges and become envious we lose our sanctity.We follow all possible means even the wrong ones to surpass our competitors, we become selfish which in no case can result in happiness.

- ***Life is a boomerang :***

Whether it is our thoughts, actions or behavior, sooner or later they return and with great accuracy. Treat people with respect on your way up because you will be meeting them on your way down.

The following story is taken from The Best of. . . Bits & Pieces.

Many years ago two boys were working their way through Stanford University. Their funds got desperately low, and the idea came to them to engage Ignacy Paderewski for a piano recital. They would use the funds to help pay their board and tuition.

The great pianist's manager asked for a guarantee of $2,000. The guarantee was a lot of money in those days, but the boys agreed and proceeded to promote the concert. They worked hard, only to find that they had grossed only $1,600. After the concert the two boys told the great artist the bad news. They gave him the entire $1,600, along with a promissory note for $400, explaining that they would earn the amount at the earliest possible moment and send the money to him. It looked like the end of their college careers.

"No, boys," replied Paderewski, "that won't do." Then, tearing the note in two, he returned the money to them as well. "Now," he told them, "take out of this $ 1,600 all of your expenses and keep for each of you 10 percent of the balance for your work.

Let me have the rest."The years rolled by. World War I came and went. Paderewski, now premier of Poland, was striving to feed thousands of starving people in his native land. The only person in the world who could help him was Herbert Hoover, who was in charge of the US Food and Relief Bureau. Hoover responded and soon thousands of tons of food were sent to Poland.

After the starving people were fed, Paderewski journeyed to Paris to thank Hoover for the relief sent him.

"That's all right, Mr. Paderewski," was Hoover's reply. "Besides, you don't remember it, but you helped me once when I was a student at college, and I was in trouble."

* Economics Press, Fairfield, NJ, 1994, pp. 84—85.

- ***The worst is yet to come:***

Just remember that there is no worse day in your life, because the worse is yet to come. Live every moment you may not get the chance to witness them again. It motivates you to live your life to fullest and prepare yourself for the worst which is yet to come. The best is yet to be enjoyed

- ***Death is destined:***

The greatest truth of life which no one wants to accept, no-one wants to face it, but we all know it's the magical truth of life.As soon as you die, your identity becomes a "body". People use phrases like "bring the body", "lower the body" "turn the body" "take the body to the graveyard". People don't even call you by your name who you tried to impress whole life. Live a life to impress creator not the creation. Live a life to express not impress.

Take chances, spend money on things you like, laugh till stomach hurts. Dance, even if you don't know. Sing even if others laugh. Pose stupid for photos. Be childlike, not childish.

"Death is not the greatest loss. Loss is when life dies before death."

- ***No two days are the same:***

Like no two persons are same, no two days are alike. Wait for the right day or make the present day perfect without leaving the opportunity to enjoy the day.This day is not going to come again at any cost. Today is great. Once lost cannot be recovered.Today makes your tomorrow better, so remember today is everything.

- ***No two individual think alike:***

Learn to live with the positive and negative sides of the people. Everyone has a darker side. Learn to live with the drawbacks of the people because no one is perfect. We cannot find anyone in complete synchronization with our thoughts and even there is no fun in that.

"Jitney log utne type ki thinking."

Taste different people, learn from them and chill out. Praise the good faculties and leave behind the bad traits.

- ***Mistakes are the stepping stones to success:***

Unless you take the first step and fall you are never going to learn to walk. Similarly, those who are afraid of committing mistakes never prosper. Let mistakes be your stepping stones in life and not the destination. Don't get stuck over them, get up and learn to move ahead. Don't be afraid to commit mistakes, don't forget to learn from them and don't dare to repeat them.

- ***You die the day you stop learning:***

It is that pedaling to our bicycle of life which, when stops us first stumble and then falls. It's like the flow of knowledge which gives out pungent smell when still. Never stop learning because age is not the criteria for learning and not even for the consistency. Questing is a key to learning

"Questioning is seductive, you can't stop once you start. And that's the way to learn."

- ***Today is the biggest truth:***

Second to death the today is the biggest truth. The past has gone to never come back again and the future hasn't yet come to be worried about. Living for today is what matters learning from the past and preparing for the future.

- ***You have to walk alone on the road to success.***

The closer you get to excellence in your life, the more friends you will lose.People love when you are average, because it makes them comfortable. But when you pursue greatness it makes them uncomfortable as filmed in the movie "3 idiots" one important part of humanPsychology

'It makes you sad when your best friend fails, but what makes one sadder is when he scores better than you"

- ***Life is a slave to desire:***

Desires are the never ending part of your life which are never going to leave you, when one is fulfilled the others are already waiting for their turn in the queue.The *biggest lie* one can say is *"I will be happy when I will get what I want"*The more we desire the more we fall slave to them and the less we can enjoy. For where there is no satisfaction there is no happy life.

Story

Once there was a foreigner who was walking through a jungle when he saw a group of elephant under a shed, tied with a very thin chain, he was confused to see that that chain is very weak and the elephants can break it easily and move away but why are they standing there as if it holding them firmly and are not even trying to move.

He waited there thinking about it when the owner of those elephants arrived there, and out of curiosity he decided to ask him the reason behind this surprising behavior of the elephants.

The owner gave a very beautiful answer. He said this is the same chain which he used to tie them when they all were very small. It was very strong for them that time and even after trying a lot they were never able to escape. And now they think that it can hold them even now so they don't even try.

This same way we humans behave. We keep worrying about the problems happened a long ago when we were weak to face them and suppose now even if we are capable of tackling them, we choose to put ourselves in front of them and don't even try and our whole life goes like this. And at the later stage when we realized this there remains nothing but the regret of the past.

Hence we should always trust our potential and keep trying because we never know when we can break the chains out and can move on to take on the world.

Once I was talking to my friend. As a topic of normal conversation we shot through that common topic of love. She asked me if am having any girlfriend. I said NO. I used to be shy, so I said "Am a bit shy, so not having many friends among girls, let's see if I get any through these years"

She simply smiled and replied "Hehe I know, I used to be like you only.Everyone has the same problem, but now am changed and a lot happier"

"Now I can fool any number of boyfriends I wish. And no worries, am enjoying and happy"

I replied "Oh wow!! We got an expert here"

She said "yeah!! Don't worry, you will learn too. And even you will be happy" I was shocked what the damn thing she was saying. Since I belong to a small town and a normal school, I never realized that these things work this way. For us even stopping by and talking to a girl was seen by the people around as some crime. They used to stare us as if we ran out of a zoo. And suddenly I had a flashback of those times and I realized that I am here in Pune, I found myself landed in completely different surroundings. I was surely going to find something extravagant and here was the start.

I was soon going to learn that the priority changes from place to place and there is a vast difference among those who live in a small village or town with a big heart and those who live in huge bungalows with education and preachings.

*Pune was certainly the place where getting a yes from a girl is far easier than getting it from a local vendor or a rickshaw driver.*As a matter of time I said" wow!! Keep guiding me with your expert opinion "and she happily agreed.

From that time I was not able to stop myself from thinking why and how it changed so much. Is it meant to be deteriorating like this? What are we giving to our future generation? A piece of shit??!

With a free and incoming enabled mind you can feel and experience many unseen things you never witnessed. You cansee hundreds of people there busy in their life with the caliber of teaching you thousands of things if you observe

I may have failed to notice little things like what the color of the door is, the shape of vase downstairs, the painting hanging and the portrait looking at me since my childhood, the graffiti written on my tee or the brand of shoe I am wearing.

But I have surely noticed the lack of conversation between two souls made for each other, lack of smileys in conversation, and the misunderstandings between people which no one else can understand better except them. The fights to prevent a relationship, tension between two people, lovers crying for each other, the extra effort from someone for the one they love, the hard work to make the parents' eyes fill with pride, the care people have for others leaving them on the stake, the hope in the eyes of a beggar.

The goodness in that child who smiles innocently looking at everyone, the courage, the pride and surely these little things makes a big picture, a picture worth noticing and a must watch. Even a trailer of this big picture can mesmerize you to live a life which it worth.

"Emotions are what that separates us from animals."

Sharing one experience

"I had one experience during my college life, I was studying in Pune, a city where the city buses running from 4am till 1am are its lifeline. And all thanks to the selfless PMT employees who never enjoy the holidays, no breaks but just work. Rakshabandhan (one of the most celebrated festivals which symbolizes the love between brother and sister.) But this PMT workers who were the reason that these brothers and sisters were able to meet each other from far across the corners of Pune didn't get a chance to be with their loved ones, As a member of one social club 'Incredible India' we felt they are our brothers as they are always there whenever we need them, we went on the main places in the city and the girls

tied rakhis on the hands of those employees, and unprecedented by such thing, unbelievably I saw tears in eyes of many people working there.

The girls responded that it was one of the most touching days to them as these PMT guys accepted them so heartedly, the pain these guys were hiding because of not being with their family on such a beautiful occasion was all gone, and one thing we were sure of is that, we were able to put some smile of their faces"

That incident clearly explained everyone of us that we all are abide by emotions. The feel which we have for each other and the love we share with each other.But there is one thing which makes me sad.

"We ignore those who adore us, adore those who ignore us, hurt those who love us and love those who hurt us"

We never appreciate those who are close to us. We ignore the efforts they put into the relationships, we ignore how beautifully they remember each and every little detail about us. But when some stranger acts well with us, we get attached to him, we start ignoring our loved ones for him. And till the time when we realize our mistake we end up losing our relationships.

"Life is like eating groundnuts. While eating, we never appreciate that they are fresh and tasty, but in case we ever happen to eat a staled one by mistake we start blaming that they all are stale and why they keep coming to our share only"

Being optimistic:

Always look for the gold in the people.*As a young boy, Andrew Carnegie came to America and started doing odd jobs. He ended up as one of the largest steel manufacturers in the United States. At one time he had 43 millionaires working for him. Several decades ago, a million dollars used to be a lot of money; even today it is a lot of money. Someone asked Mr. Carnegie how he dealt with people? Andrew Carnegie replied, "Dealing with people is like digging gold: When you go digging for an ounce of gold, you have to move tons of dirt to get an ounce of gold. But when you go digging, you don't go looking for the dirt, you go looking for the gold."*

To sum up everything we learned until now, let me tell you a short story

When I was a small boy, my mother told me that being happy is the key to life. When I went to school they told me to write what I want to be when I grow up. I wrote 'Happy'. My teacher questioned me that she didn't understand my assignment and I replied that "you didn't understand life"

But now we have to introspect ourselves, because though we know much about the world we know very little about us. Discovering ourselves will only help us to attain the life we dream of and it will help us to irradiate the darkness that lies within.

"Sometimes instead of striving hard to find the light everywhere you go, it is better to carry your own sunshine"

The simple seven of life

1) Before you pray- believe
2) Before you speak- listen
3) Before you spend- earn
4) Before you write- think
5) Before you quit- try
6) Before you die- live
7) Before you hate- learn to love

Why Complicate life

Missing somebody: Call
Want to meet up: Invite
Want to be understood: Explain
Have questions: Ask
Don't like something: Say it
Like something: State it
Want something: Ask for it
Love someone: Tell it
We just have one life, keep it simple

Life is an opportunity, benefit from it. Life is beauty, admire it.

Life is a dream, realize it. Life is a challenge, meet it. Life is a duty, complete it. Life is a game, play it. Life is a promise, fulfil it.

Life is sorrow, overcome it. Life is a song, sing it.

Life is a struggle, accept it. Life is a tragedy, confront it. Life is an adventure, dare it. Life is luck, make it.

Life is too precious, do not destroy it. Life is life, fight for it."

–Mother Teresa

EXPLORING YOURSELF

"Anyone can **be a winner** *with the help of world's greatest freedom. The freedom to be the best."*

The life lesson from the empty pickle jar

Once a philosophy professor enters the class with an empty pickle jar. He asked students what they can see. The students answered that a pickle jar. He further asked whether the jar is empty. The students replied "The jar is empty". The professor then took some golf balls and put them one by one in the glass jar to fill it. He again asked his students to tell that whether the jar is empty or filled up. The student's answers that the jar is now full. The professor searched under his table and took out some pebbles. He then put those pebbles inside that jar. The pebbles covered the empty space. The class was looking at the professor what he was trying to do.

When the professor asked again, whether the jar was empty or full. The students replied "Yes! Now the jar is full" the professor said "hmm!! Oh. Let's see, " he then took some sand and poured it in the jar. Now the sand took the complete remaining portion of the space left. He looked at the class again and asked the same question. The class gave the same answer, but this time with less confidence. The professor then took some coconut milk and poured inside the jar, and it too occupied the space.The class started laughing.

Now the professor told the class to imagine and compare the glass jar as their family. The golf balls are all those important things in their life that matter them the most. Like the family, children, health. The pebbles are the next important things like money job career. He further addressed that the sand is the remaining things in the life and the problems that matter less.

He said 'If we fill our lives first with coconut milk or sand or pebbles, then we won't have space for those things that matter us the most."

One and all we are bored,

Deep in our thoughts we are soared.

Waiting for the time to turn the chime,

Waiting for the train in the dripping rain.

We wait for the letters

That won't get better.

We cry our tears, forgetting the cheers.

We play dumb, on the issues numb.

Out there, there is an everyday battle,

But our issues weight with us at the castle.

We feel pain in our knees,

Rot our relations like a cheese.

Still dance we do, to hide our pain,

With that rotten cheese, one ain't gonna gain.

We should first be able to distinguish between the things that we want and the things that matters us the most. And that is possible only by gaining wisdom. Once we realize what we actually need, we can make our move to achieve it.

So how to achieve that wisdom? Here is a beautiful story that will make it simpler.

A young man asked Socrates, how he could get wisdom. Socrates replied, "Come with me." He took the lad to the river, pushed the boy's head under water and held it there until the boy was gasping for air. Then he relaxed and released his head. When the boy regained his composure, he asked him, 'What were there you wanted most when you were under water?"

"I wanted air," said the boy.
Socrates then said to him,

"When you want wisdom as much as you wanted air when you were under water, you will get it" Likewise, when we really have an intense desire to overcome any block in our life and we come to a clear cut decision that there is a way that can lead us out of the trouble and that is the course that we have to follow then the victory and triumph is surely ours and no force in the universe can prevent us fromgetting that no matter what comes in the way.

When we really want peace and internal calm, we will get it, regardless of how unjust and improper we are treated and how bad time we have been through. No matter how unjust the life has been, no matter how the scoundrel (crook) someone has proved to be, it doesn't matter how much loss you are in. It makes no difference to you when you are mentally and spiritually awaken to your powers. When we know what we want and how important that is for us, we automatically prevent all those bad and negative thoughts, hatred, anger, hostility (opposition or aggression), and ill to rob us of peace, harmony, happiness and eventually success.

When we have all this in mind that we want to be happy and we want to achieve that one goal, we automatically stop being upset by our surrounding and environment, we stop getting angry on small things, we automatically cease letting people affect our thought process. When our aim is peace and harmony, when our aim is happiness and calmness, we automatically start feelinglike the flowing river of peace and inspiration that makes its way through the toughest and hardest rocks and mountain. That gets adapt to its surrounding and cleans every negative thought coming its way but never stops. We become that lively river, because when we know what we want and have a complete trust over it, we achieve it.

When you are on your quest to achieve this wisdom, you should…

Promise Yourself -

- That you will be so strong that nothing can disturb your peace of mind.

- To talk health, happiness, and prosperity to every person you meet.
- To make all your friends feel that there is something in them
- To look at the sunny side of everything and make your optimism come true
- To think only the best, to work only for the best, and to expect only the best.
- To be just as enthusiastic about the success of others as you are about your own.
- To forget the mistakes of the past
- And press on to the greater achievements of the future.
- To wear a cheerful countenance at all times and give every living creature you meet a smile.
- To give so much time to the improvement of yourself that you have no time to criticize others.
- To be too large for worry, too noble for anger, too strong for fear, and too happy to permit the presence of trouble.
- To think well of yourself and to proclaim this fact to the world, not in loud words but great deeds.
- To live in faith that the whole world is on your side so long as you are true to the best that is in you."

After you promise yourself all these and you decide to do something extraordinary and different and when you want to swim opposite to flow when you just don't want to sit there and relax and when thousands of thoughts are pricking your mind, when you want to stand up high there are something you have to sacrifice. There are some habits you have to leave behind. There are some thoughts you need to change. There are some habits you need to forget there are moments when you have to stop being satisfied for little and there are situations when you have to crave more, demand the world, order from its menu list.

The story of Tortoise and Rabbit

This is an age old fable of the tortoise and hare race. Everyone knows who won the race or do you? Well, recently I heard a new version of this story during my college with a new twist. Read this inspirational teamwork story with lessons in teamwork from an age old fable.

1. Once upon a time a tortoise and a hare had an argument about who was faster. They decided to settle the argument with a race. The tortoise and hare both agreed on a route and started off the race. The hare shot ahead and ran briskly for some time. Then, seeing that he was far ahead of the tortoise, he thought he'd sit under a tree for some time and relax before continuing the race. He sat under the tree and soon fell asleep. The tortoise plodding on overtook him and soon finished the race, emerging as the undisputed champ. The hare woke up and realized that he'd lost the race.The moral of the story is that **slow and steady wins the race**. This is the version of the story that we've all grown up with.

2. But then recently, someone told me a more interesting version of this tortoise and hare story. It continues.

   The hare was disappointed at losing the race and he did some soul-searching. He realized that he'd lost the race only because he had been overconfident, careless and lax. If he had not taken things for granted, there's no way the tortoise could have beaten him. So he challenged the tortoise to another race. The tortoise agreed.

   This time, the hare has gone all out and ran without stopping from start to finish. He won by several miles.

   The moral of the story? **In business, fast and consistent will always beat the slow and steady**. If you don't act with a sense of urgency you will get left behind.

3. But the story doesn't end here. The tortoise has done some thinking this time, and realized that there's no way he can beat the hare in a race the way it was currently formatted. He thought

for a while, and then challenged the hare to another race, but on a slightly different route. The hare agreed. The tortoise and hare started off. In keeping with his self-made commitment to be consistently fast, the hare took off and ran at top speed until he came to a broad river. The finishing line was a couple of kilometers on the other side of the river.

The hare sat there wondering what to do. In the meantime the tortoise trundled along, got into the river, swam to the opposite bank, continued walking and finished the race.

The moral of the story? **Don't over-analyze and over-think. Just take action. Learn about your competitors, identify their weakness and play smart.**

The story still doesn't end here.

4. The tortoise and hare, by this time, had become pretty good friends and they did some thinking together. Both realized that the last race could have been run much better. So the tortoise and hare decided to do the last race again, but run as a team this time.

They started off, and this time the hare carried the tortoise till the riverbank. There, the tortoise took over and swam across with the hare on his back. On the opposite bank, the hare again carried the tortoise and they reached the finishing line together. Both the tortoise and hare felt a greater sense of satisfaction than they'd felt earlier.

The moral of the story? **Teamwork works.** It's good to be individually brilliant; but unless you're able to work with a team and harness each other's core strengths, you'll always perform below par because there will always be situations at which you'll do poorly and someone else does well.

"The Disease of Me can lead to The Defeat of US"

Note that neither the tortoise nor hare gave up after failures. The hare decided to work harder and put in more effort after his failure. The tortoise changed his strategy because he was already working as hard as he could.

In life, when faced with failure, sometimes it is appropriate to work harder and put in more effort.

Sometimes it is appropriate to change strategy and try something different. And sometimes it is appropriate to do both. Maybe in your current situation you are always working hard, but never winning the race. Maybe it's time to look back and change your strategy.

Learn about your core competencies. Develop yourselves collectively. Our happiness lies in working together and it lies in happiness of everyone.

For those who only learned the mantra of *slow and steady wins the race,* they need to know that there are many things out in the world which we are yet to learn.

"The Only Thing That Is Constant Is Change"

-Heraclitus

Just following the school and rule books is going to take us nowhere. We need to consistently adapt to changes and make improvements.

"It is not the strongest species that survive, nor the most intelligent, but the ones most responsive to change."

- Charles Darwin

What we see and what we hear is not the truth always. Only an exploring mind can identify a diamond from the coal. Am not saying don't trust what you learned. Just don't be satisfied about it only.

Just being fast is not enough. You need a direction and consistency. A bullet fired from the best gun by the most skillful hand is wastage if it doesn't have a proper direction. Similarly, if you don't have consistency, it will take no time even for a looser to overcome you and leave you thinking how stupid you were.

Going to the field without knowing your opponents, their powers and weakness is like going to snake and putting a gun on his head forcing him to bite you.

Lord Buddha said, "You are the community. Be a lamp for yourselves. Be your own refuge seek for no other all things must pass strive on diligently. Don't give up. Embrace nothing. Only live your life as it is. Not bound to anything! However many holy words you read however many you speak. What good will they do you if you do not act on upon them?

You can search throughout the entire universe for someone who is more deserving of your love and affection than you are yourself, and that person is not to be found anywhere you yourself, as much as anybody in the entire universe, deserve your love and affection. To be idle is a short road to death. And to be diligent is a way of life: foolish people are idle, wise people are diligent. In the sky there is no distinction of East and West: people create distinctions out of their own minds, and then believe them to be true Peace comes from within."

Elements of human psychology

The Subconscious you

Have you ever wondered why one man is sad and another one is happy? Why one man is joyous and prosperous and another man is poor and miserable? Why one man is fearful and anxious and another man is full of faith and confidence? Why does one man have a beautiful, luxurious home while the other lives in meager existence in the slums? Why one man gets everything, even if he never ask God for it and why another man who always prays to god gets only misery? Why one man a great success and another is just a symbol of failure? Why one man is an outstanding speaker while the other just can't take a single word out in public? Why one man is the success symbol and another is a blot of failure? Why one man is immensely popular and another man is second -rate and unpopular? Why one man is a genius in his work while the other toils and moils just to get his recognition the whole life? Why one woman is happy with her lover while the other is under frustration and about to be separated? Why immoral people succeed and enjoy while the moral one suffers the torture of stress and unhappiness in their soul and body?

From- The power of your subconscious mind.

Have you ever asked yourself just a Why?? What you think can be the reason behind this inequality. All these people are same like me and you of flesh and blood like yours and mine, then why there is so uncertainty? What could be the probable reason!!

The answer lies here. Yes, they're only deep inside you. It's all because of the thought process and the actions you take, the people who are happy and prosperous are those who do those things and have that approach which the weak and unhappy people try to avoid.

Our chemistry teacher once told a beautiful story of a famous chemist during the college. It beautifully describes the power of the subconscious mind.

Friedrich Von Stradonitz, used the subconscious mind to solve a problem that was troubling him since long. He had been working laboriously for a long time trying to rearrange the six carbon and the six hydrogen atoms of the benzene formula. He was constantly perplexed (confused) and unable to solve the problem. Tired and exhausted, he turned the request completely to his subconscious mind. Shortly afterwards, when he was about to board train to London bus, his subconscious mind presented his conscious mind with a sudden flash of a snake biting its own tail and turning around like a pin wheel. This answer, from his subconscious mind, gave him long sought answer of the circular arrangement of the atoms that is today known as benzene ring.

So who can take the benefit of this approach? Yes! Anyone.

"Our subconscious minds have no sense of humor, play no jokes and cannot tell the difference between reality and an imagined thought or an image. What we continually think about will come true and manifest our lives. "

- Robert Collier

Whatever we plant in our subconscious mind and nourish it with repetition and emotions will one day become the reality.

Realize and learn how powerful your thoughts are. Because once you realize the same you will never dare to think of a negative one.

Our subconscious mind is driven by few simple elements like,

- **Narrow mindedness**
- **Fear**
- **Anger**

These first three elements are negative aspects of life. But they can be overcome by,

- **Belief**
- **Faith**
- **Hope**

Let's take a look at each one of them one by one

Narrow Mindedness

Signs that you are narrow minded

- You don't like anyone who disagrees with you.
- You keep presuming things.
- You always want to be right.
- You keep thinking people are playing games with you.
- You make a generalized decision about anyone and anything without knowledge.
- You find hard to interact with people when you mind any shortcoming in them.
- You keep contacts with people only because you need them.
- You find it difficult to connect with people around you easily.
- You usually don't express yourself.
- You care too much what people think and try being fake.
- You like to pinpoint the negativity of events, people, and personality.
- Your old and rusted beliefs don't allows you to accept the truth.
- You live in a bubble where your life is the only world.
- You hide your progress, because you think that if you showcase it the others will outpace you.

Narrow-minded people don't like new ideas; they cling desperately to their own way of thinking. They think they're always right and have no qualms about attacking anyone who contradicts them.

They're almost always outdated, stuck in time.They refuse to better themselves and refuse to consider other people's point of view.

In some way, we are all narrow-minded. No one is perfectly open-minded about everything.

How does open-mindedness work? How can you get smarter without becoming more narrow-minded? Let's look at a few things that can help:

Read more. Be selective in your reading. Don't read anything that makes you upset, bored or makes you feel useless. If you like photography, read the magazines. If you like business, read stories that inspire you.

Travel. Travelling helps to open up your mind. We learn to look at things with different aspects. You may not be able to fly to Tokyo, but it's amazing how many new things we can discover on the other side of the city we live in, or in a nearby city.

Inspire not discourage. Narrow minded people feels that to excel they need to put down the others. Learn that

"You can't **achieve** *success by rubbing the existing line, but only by drawing a* **bigger** *one next to it."*

Praise people for what they are, try to understand them. Stop criticizing and start celebrating.

Listen More. Narrow minded people usually don't like to listen. They just want themselves to talk. When they wish to listen it's just about themselves. They keep making a script in mind about what to say next. But force yourself to listen. One learns a lot that way.

Upgrade your Friendship:

"Birds of a feather flock together"

We learn the same we feel and we listen. Our surroundings have an effect on us. We become what our friends are. Narrow minded friends can prove poisonous. Take them out before they hurt you. Be with those who inspire you to be stronger and better.

Learn from Great Thinkers. Start with the top thinker, and then work your way down. By learning from Him, you'll safeguard yourself from being open-minded for what is bad.

Stop judging and starts loving. Work at understanding things and people before passing judgment.

"Love for what they are and not for what you want them to be"

Take Actions. People tend to think a lot but they hardly take actions. Remember

"There is a difference between even I could do that and I did it"

Watch documentaries. Leave those soap operas and reality shows behind. They are scripted to stagnant your thinking abilities,narrow your views. They don't add up to anything in life, but makes you fall a victim of nonsense and stupidity. They waste your time. Documentaries from reputable sources, e.g. BBC, Discovery, History Channel, etc. Are excellent ways of travelling without even getting up from the sofa.

Narrow mindedness can even lead you to fear.

Fear

Forget Everything and Run

Or

Fight Everything and Rise

Fear-simply stated as the man's greatest enemy, but here I would like to mention that when it comes to our greatest enemy, I would like to readdress it as the biggest tutor and the greatest inspiration.

*"In the **practice** of tolerance and **courage** one's enemy can be his greatest inspiration"*

An enemy can teach you those things you can never thought exists and never expects any of your tutor and nor the parents to teach you ever in life.

A man goes through many fears. Fears of losing that may be your battle, your exam, a game or a loved one. Fear may be about death. Fear may be of being unsuccessful, fear of failing and the list continues.

> *"Our deepest* ***fear is*** *not that we are* ***inadequate****. Our deepest* ***fear is*** *that we are* ***powerful*** *beyond measure. It is our light, not our darkness that most frightens us. We ask ourselves, 'Who am I to be brilliant, gorgeous, talented, and fabulous?' Actually, who are you not to be? You are a child of God. You're playing small does not serve the world."*
>
> *- Marianne Williamson, A Return to Love: Reflections on the Principles of "A Course in Miracles"*

Fear surrounds us all, right from waking up to the time we sleep. It controls our mind all the time. Even when we are happy a fear surrounds us. It makes us think "What if this moment ends? What will I do after this?" When we are with our loved ones some feels "What is this relationship won't last? What if he/she leaves me alone?" Some people fear hard work. Like some fear failure, there are also those who fear success also. The fear of success makes you feel unsatisfied even you achieve it. I don't mean a single successful attempt should be your destination, we should keep moving forward, but one should enjoy every single bit of it. Such people fail to enjoy and spoils the mood of life. They simply fail to live.Sometimes the power and the urge of the negative thoughts can break the power of positive thoughts.

Sometimes the fear to die can make you live longer than the urge to live. When you fear something you automatically starts to run your mechanism to overcome it and to make yourself free from that fear. And there your action starts. Suppose a man is running behind you with a gun in hand to shoot you, that time you have to run like hell to save yourself, you have to run hard and nonstop only then you can save yourself, at such cases the fear of death helps instead of the urge that you want to live.

How to overcome fear? Can anyone be brave? How to be brave?

"Bran thought about It. ' can a **man** *still* **be** *brave if he's afraid?'*

'That is the only time a man can be **brave,**' *his father told him."*

¯George R.R. Martin, A Game of Thrones

Veronica Roth says that there are so many ways to be brave in this world. Sometimes bravery involves laying down your life for something bigger than yourself, or for someone else. Sometimes it involves giving up everything you have ever known, or everyone you have ever loved, for the sake of something great. But sometimes it doesn't.Sometimes it is nothing more than gritting your teeth through pain, and the work of everyday, the slow walk toward a better life.

Five steps to develop courage

- Face up reality.
- Re-examine your value system and take a stand.
- Build character.
- Practise small act of courage.
- Perfect practise leads to preparation.

*"***Courage** *is not the absence of fear, but rather the judgement that something else* **is** *more* **important** *than fear."*

- Ambrose Redmoon

Anger

Anger, this concept is as easy as it is difficult.

When you get angry what you feel the most is that it should get attention from someone, especially the one at whom you are getting angry. And if it is not working your anger increases.

Sometimes anger is for showing care, sometimes it's just for asking more attention sometimes demanding love. It's naturally an easy and immature way to show all such feelings **the emotion of anger** is yet a bit complicated and if taken as a subject of study it can disappoint us. Because we will realize not matter how hard, no matter how long and no matter on whom you remain angry, most of the time it goes in vain.

Because when you get angry on someone even you know it's not going to last forever. No matter what the reason. You and that person both are going to be happy and going to forget what was the past and why were you angry. So if you think a little what was the use if it's not going to be remembered and cared? You just wasted some beautiful movements of life in getting angry, which literally got no future.

I learned this when I was just a kid who use to be very demanding and was not ever ready to accept a NO about anything he demanded. My father use to know it and he knew that if he is going to say NO to anything I will go on strike, no food no milk and eventually end up emotionally blackmailing my mother.. He always use to reply a yes to any of my demands no matter what I demanded. So that at least at that time the mood of everyone especially mine can be stabilized.

But when he doesn't use to fulfil some of my irrelevant demands I basically use to get angry, throwing tantrums, not eating food (probably a child's best revenge against parents), not talking to anyone properly and my dad just uses to sit and relax, read his newspaper, solve crosswords while my mom on the other hand use to get upset that her son is not eating and is upset on us. Which used to ignite me more and act as oil in my fire of anger. I don't know why, but it use to add to my *stupidity*. But my dad used to be calm. I then realized what the use of this anger when he (from whom my demands are to be met) is not even responding to it.

I realized he was busy doing his work and happy. It felt as if he ignored my anger and am holding my anger like an idiot.

'The ***science*** *of ignoring the ignorance* ***can't be*** *ignored while being* ***ignored"***

Being an idiot I use to keep this situation going for minimum 2days. 1st day dad don't uses to interfere much so that things don't get worse, but 2nd day when I am still troubling myself by not enjoying my favorite food and cartoon shows, when I am still busy being stupid and holding grudges, he use to come to me and used to pamper me. He started being normal, talking normally as if nothing has happened yesterday and you can still see me on the sofa with anger on my face. I use to feel like a fool. I use to long this session of anger, but in vain. He use to talk normally to me and I use to waste my time.

From that I learned that anger is such a waste of time. You land up wasting your own moments of happiness that too without anything in return.

There may be two cases

1) Either the other person doesn't care about your anger
2) He cares and hence start acting normally the next time hoping that things are now normal, but you still find yourself wasting all the awesome things around you in holding grudges that got no use.

Story:

There once was a little boy who had a bad temper. His father gave him a bag of nails and told him that every time he lost his temper, he must hammer a nail into the fence. The first day the boy had driven 37 nails into the fence. Over the next few weeks, as he learned to control his anger, the number of nails hammered daily, gradually dwindled down. He discovered it was easier to hold his temper than to drive those nails into the fence.

Finally the day came when the boy didn't lose his temper at all. He told his father about it and the father suggested that the boy now pull out one nail for each day that he was able to hold his temper. The days passed and the young boy was finally able to tell his father that all the nails were gone.

The father took his son by the hand and led him to the fence. He said "you have done well, my son, but look at the holes in the fence. The fence will never be the same. When you say things in anger, they leave a scar just like this one." You can put a knife in a man and draw it out. It won't matter how many times you say I'm sorry, the wound is still there. Make sure you control your temper the next time you are tempted to say something or you will regret later.

The things actually start getting complicated when you start understanding more about something.

What's happened in my case many times is that knowing the above fact, I never wanted my anger go to waste so I always tried to retain it so that the third person can realize about it and make the necessary action, more and more time was spent getting angry in an attempt to make the person notice it.

But at the end you have to leave it back. You waste your time, your energy and your anger.

Always remember

*"**Anger** is an acid that **can** do more **harm** to the vessel in which it is stored than to **anything** on which it is poured."*

–Mark Twain

Belief

An unbelievable story of Belief

There was a girl name of Wilma Rudolph. Born immaturely in a black family, her weight being two kilograms at the time of her birth. She was crippled by polio during her childhood. One doctor told her mother that the condition couldn't be cured. But the doctor's verdict wouldn't affect the mother. Wilma says while bringing back the memories of her childhood, 'the doctor said I would never walk again, my mother said I would. And I believed my mother. Wilma's mother found out there is one hospital some eight kilometers from her place where her daughter could be treated. She took her daughter twice a week for two years an end. After two years treatment Wilma was able to walk with the help of crutches.

Finally, at the age of twelve, she began walking normally without crutches.

At the age of sixteen, in the 1956 Olympics, she won a bronze in 4x4 relay.In the 1960 Olympics, she became the first American woman to win three gold in the Olympics.

*"**Our** attempts may be awkward. Our attempts may be feeble. But since the **power** of our attempts **liesin** the **passion** and dedication we do it and not the one who does it, our attempts do make a difference."*

So what is faith? *True faith is much more than just believing.* The dictionary says

Belief - *An opinion or judgement in which a person is fully persuaded.*
Faith- *(Belief + Action + Confidence)*

While 'faith' surely includes the element of 'belief', they are not one and the same. Certainly one must believe that something, or someone, exists before it is possible to put one's faith in that person or thing. However, I can believe some things that do not affect my life. I believe China exists, but I do not live my life any differently because of my belief. This type of 'belief' is not true faith.

To put one's 'faith' in something, or someone, means that one is putting his or her trust in that person or thing. Who or what one trusts can have far-reaching, even eternal, ramifications. It means relying on, depending upon, that person or thing. Let's take an example. Suppose I am standing on a cliff and I wish to jump off. I believe if I try I can do it. But I am afraid of jumping. It reveals that though I believe it can be done, I don't have faith in myself. Also, if I don't jump I can't blame for missing the adventure I might have experienced. I must have faith and jump to explore what is there for me.

Faith

There once lived a man who seemed to have lot of faith in God, he used to worship daily. He had a belief that he can't be ever be caught in any problem since he is so close to God and someday even if he does get caught then also no worries as his god will run to his help.

Unfortunately, one day the town where he used to live got struck with heavy flood, all the houses were collapsing, roads were jammed, and even this man was stuck somewhere in some building. As he came to know about the flood, he came out of his room and walked towards the terrace.

People were advising him that there is still a chance they can escape but he rejected and said no you creatures go, my god will save me and went at the top of

terrace to see what's going on. He was looking at the people suffering from flood "poor people, what are they going through. But I don't have to worry my god will save me" it took no time for the water to reach his area. The water slowly started rising, since it was very strong and the tallest building he was feeling safe. The water now started filling the groundfloor he was still standing there.

He saw few men coming near a building to lend a helping hand. They shouted "Come with us, we got a safe place." He answered back "No thanks, my God will save me" they tried to convince him but in vain and they left. The water now reached the first floor and this man was still standing there. He saw a tire tube coming near the building, he still didn't made a move thinking that his god will save him, later as the water reached the second floor the structure of building shackled, a lifeboat with some military man came near him, but he rejected their help too, because of same reason, soon a helicopter approached him, but he yelled at them "Why don't you poor people understand?, I don't need anyone's help, my God will save me." But to his misery the building collapsed and the fellow died.

He found himself before God for execution, he got angry at him and shouted "You!! I trusted you, why didn't you save me? I used to pray like hell in front of you, you deceived me, I don't trust you now"The god calmly replied "Son, take a Second and try to understand who send all those help to you"The man ran into shock with complete silence as he realized his mistake.

Moral: He trusted God, that's good, but a blind faith can harm you, he saw the opportunities coming he should understand that he have to help himself

"Hath lagaye bina badhti nai gaadi kaamki, kuch hota nai bas deke duhai ram ki"

It means that if one just keep chanting god's name instead of doing any work, he is going nowhere.

*"**Faith** is not the belief that God will do what you want. It **is** the belief that **God** will do what is right."*

– Max Lucado, He Still Moves Stones

The story of a mountain

Once a woman came across the following verse from the bible.

'If you have ***faith*** *as a grain of mustard seed, you shall say unto this mountain,* ***remove*** *hence to yonder place, and it shall remove and nothing shall be* ***impossible*** *to you"*

Upon reading this, intrigues by curiosity, she decided to check out if this is true. So the same night before going to bed, she commanded the mountain through the window of her room, thus 'leave the place where you are now and move yourself one kilometer behind. It's okay if you take your time and do so anytime till dawn'

Upon waking up when she looked through the window, she saw no change, the mountain was standing there where it was there last night and hadn't moved.

She was not much surprised. She was doubtful enough already about the possibility of a mountain moving to yonder place.

She said, 'I knew that, how can a mountain move?'

Irrespective of who thinks what, faith remains the power that moves mountains and more, even if its quantity is as small as a grain of mustard seed.

Faith in yourself can do miracle

"All the world is made of faith, and trust, and pixie dust."

– J.M. Barrie, Peter Pan

There is a fine line between faith and fear. That is called doubt.

"Doubt separates people. It is a poison that disintegrates friendships and breaks up pleasant relations. It is a thorn that irritates and hurts, it is a sword that kills."

Paulo Coelho said "One must be careful never to allow doubt to paralyze you. Always take the decisions you need to take, even if you're not sure you're doing the right thing. You'll never go wrong if, when you make a decision, you keep in mind an old German proverb: 'The devil is in the detail.' Remember that proverb and you'll always be able to turn a wrong decision into a right one."

"When men gets over his fear and doubt, when he has **faith** *in himself, then he realizes what he* **is capable** *of"*

Hope

Once upon a time there were four candles. The four candles slowly burned. The ambiance was so soft that one could almost hear them talking. The first candle said: "I am peace; the world is full of anger. Nobody can keep me lit" than the flame of peace went out completely. The second candle said, "I am faith, I am no longer indispensable. It doesn't make sense that I stay lit another moment" just then the breeze blew the flame softly. The third candle sadly began to speak "I am love, people no longer understand my importance and keep me aside. They even forget to love those who are close to them" and waiting no longer the love candle went out. Suddenly a small kid entered the room and was surprised to see the three candles were not burning. He astonishingly asked that "Why are you three not burning, you three are supposed to be lit till the end" saying this the child began to cry.

Then the fourth candle answered. "Don't be afraid my child, I am Hope. While I am still burning you can relight the three candles" with shining eyes and smiling faces and rubbing his hands to put away the tears the child pick the candle of hope and lit those three candles.

The greatest of these is love. But the flame of hope should never go out of life. With hope we can love with peace.

The hope stays forever, its eternal, its immortal.

"When you have lost **hope**, *you have lost* **everything**. *And when you think all is lost, when all is dire and bleak, there is always hope."*

–Pittacus Lore, I Am Number Four

There remains one more element. It is called as Love. But since it is a very vast concept, we will study it as a different chapter altogether.

We can feel and we can ex press

We can accept and yes, we can protest

We can love and we can hate

But feeling nothing is not our fate.

We live once and the death is certain,

Still, we keep our eyes closed with curtains.

We know the world but we don't know us,

*Yes we feel the love when life comes to *kuss.*

We are not here just to breathe

The knife is not meant to be forever in sheathe

We are here to discover our calling

We are humans to help the society from falling.

(* Kuss- to touch with lips usually to express affection)

"Anyone can **be a winner** *with the help of world's greatest freedom. The freedom to be the best."*

LOVE - A WEIRD CONCEPT

*"**Love is** like jumping off a very tall building, where your mind says it's not a **good** idea, but your heart says you can do it."*

About falling in love we belong to that generation that may have recorded the maximum number of falls. But still it's true thatbefore it happens you walk the roads like a lone ranger, standing tall and proud, being hard and harsh, and a man thinking everything from a brain keeping heart away from the game. Then suddenly you encounter a smiling face across your territory, enjoying every moment, going hand in hand with the life, cherished, flawless face. And you suddenly lose your heart there.

You look at her and fall in love and she smiles because she knew. A *dhak dhak* starts to occur in the heart. You can do nothing, but think about that person the whole day and in each dream. You got to know them. You have to, because you know it's not going to work anymore without them no matter how tough you are on the outside. Automatically when that once the unknown face you never ever recognized before, which you used to just see passing you by starts to control everything in and around you. Everything you feel, everything you see, everything you want, feels like having some unbreakable bond with that person since ages.

"One life, one girl, one song, one love, one dream"

The person controls everything: Your feelings, your thoughts, your views and your dreams. You still a lone ranger no doubt, you still walk the road with pride, but now it feels incomplete and useless.

It's senseless to walk around like a fool without that one person. Everything you need is to complete yourself and everything you want is to be with that person only.

"You know you're in ***love*** *when you can't fall asleep because* ***reality*** *is finally better than your dreams."*

You are still selfish, but now this selfishness encircle not you but that person. You can do anything to keep that person safe, happy. You are selfish because you can do anything to make that person smile, because it's her smile that automatically drain all the sorrows from your face and makes you feel completely free. But now that's love and being this selfish is not wrong, is it?

Just seeing her smile with her friends somewhere long automatically makes you smile and sometimes it's just this smile that teaches many fundamentals and basics of life which many great books failed to. Suddenly it makes us feel that our life got a goal, a motto, and a responsibility to stick by, to live for. When you smile back after she smiles at you is that moment you actually start stepping into something different aspect of life and prepare yourself for the future to make yourself capable of standing up to the responsibility of everyone.

It's the time when you change completely. Before that the existence of someone around you used to feel nothing but existence of someone of the same species and race as yours, but know the aspect starts to change. It's the time when you start respecting every feeling and every emotion. It's the time when the tough guy inside you is tough only for those who messes with your girl.

Being a gentleman becomes the first goal. When her likes becomes your likes and her dislikes becomes your foe. When no matter where you are, what you are doing, each and everything reminds you of her face, which you saw smiling in crowd past back then when you fall in her love with no intention.

Songs remind you of her voice when passing a florist each and every flower seems to be waiting for her only. Looking outside your window during a pleasant evening makes you see nothing but her with her head on your shoulder and your fingers through her hair making out the most beautiful conversation that could ever happen.

When looking at her face makes you feel like in heaven, her voice sounds better than *Beethoven*. Her anger feels cute. The desperation you have when you are not talking to her for a single moment. When you *need* more than any of your needs a single moment without her feels like you have been waiting for ages. The desperation she shows for you makes you feel no less than *a Bollywood* hero.

The way she looks back at you after saying a bye. The way she turns around to see just a glimpse of you last time before she goes to sleep. The way her flicks comes on her cheeks, the way she raises her shoulder and smile back at you are those moments which one can never forget.

Walking through the streets with her in a rainy season under the same umbrella when she puts her head on your shoulder and you enjoy the cold breeze and the moment when the winds start to blow and she puts down the umbrella, moves out and spreads her hand under the falling drops of rain and starts stomping in the puddles. The moment when you look at her and smile and she comes running towards you and pulls you with her.

That could possibly the only time when getting wet under the rain will not irritate you and instead of cursing, you will thank God for the rain and may be the only time after your childhood you enjoyed getting yourself drenched in water .Love is when a voice whispers in your heart *"Tu nai to lage mera koi bhi nai"*

The time after the moment when she brings out the kid in you, you both walk towards home with shoes in your hand, wet clothes, lost umbrella, sneezing, feeling cold, when she rubs her shoulder with her hand to get some warmth and you take outyour jacket and puts it over her shoulder and she hugs you back.

*"**Love** is when you look at **your girl** and realize that why it didn't work with anyone else and why it will never be."*

Love is not when you are just attracted towards someone, you enjoy their company. Because there are many with whom you can enjoy and feel better when they are around. But love is for that one person you can't enjoy and you can't live without.

Love is when you and your girl are standing at the top of a very tall building close to each other. She is holding your hand firmly like the little one holds their parents, where she looks into your eyes and you can see the spark which clearly says that there is no one else in the world who can love you more than her. It's when you both look down that tall building and see the sparkling city, flooded with people, bathing with pleasing light. There is no limit to the view, as far as you can see there are vehicles, the honk of the horn, people walking around, flashing lights, the hoardings, the hawkers, children playing around, tea stalls, couples living their moments.

All you see is a world that is totally unknown of your presence and is living their own destiny, enjoying their moments, and at that time when you hug her tightly and press her palm. When you talk to her at the beautiful location, it feels like you both are above everyone else, it doesn't matter what the world does or what people do, you don't care whether the world is still, it's moving or is at a halt. All that matters is you to her and she to you the relation where has gone far from anyone's thinking and is not a 'dependent 'of this world

Doesn't it feels beautiful to be in the world where you think nobody cares, there is a person who cares just for you, a person who concentrates just on you, who walks for you, rests for you, a person who takes his every breathe just to be with you, isn't it beautiful to know and have the feeling that someone loves you, isn't it beautiful to have someone who thinks just about you, the feeling when you realize that someone is waiting for your call, isn't it beautiful who knowingly goes on a fast because you are on one. Won't that feel awesome to have your name in someone's personal diary which he always keeps close to his heart under the pillow, the feeling when someone moves his hand over your photo look at it with a different glow in his eyes, smile like an idiot and hugs the photo touches it to his heart and slowly whispers 'I love you', having someone for whom your tears are worth more than pearls.

"Sometimes when you can't stop **thinking about** *someone it is because there are chances that even they are missing* **you***"*

And after all what can you expect from two fools, nothing but pure and innocent love. If you can answer why you love him/her it's simply not love there is one act that sums it up all. The act of 'romance', the act that binds the two hearts, two souls for the infinite time and beyond, this is that act which sees no age, no boundaries, it knows no barriers, romance at the age 90 can make you feel so young as in the age 16.

Teasing your wife at 90s, or romancing with your girl at 16 is nowhere different till it maintains its purity, it's all about purity, romance doesn't mean sex, and if it means, it means in pure form, It's something that is apart from lust, the feel it brings, the sensations that run through the body, the bond that is established and the memories you make last forever.

When you are with someone romance is what that completes you, a mere expression of feelings, or mere kiss on the neck or doing as small as taking something so sweet takes the relationship to a higher level of completion

You realize it's not love when you are with a girl, enjoying her company and suddenly remember there used to be a girl with whom you enjoyed the same, and there are some other friends of yours with whom you will feel the same.Because *there is a difference between thinking someone is cute, having a crush on someone, being interested in someone, liking someone, having a desire to live with someone, loving someone and being in love with someone.*

*"There is a difference between having only single person in your life and hence he/ **she** means everything to you and not letting anyone mean to you anything when he/ she **is** in your **life**"*

"Love is patient, love is kind. It does not envy, it does not boast, it is not proud. It is not rude, it is not self-seeking, and it is not easily angered, and it keeps no record of wrongs. Love does not delight in evil but rejoices with the truth. It always protects, always trusts, always hopes, and always perseveres."

Love is not something with a happy ending. Because happy ending is just not the right term to describe it, it has no ending. Love is forever. *Because if it's not forever, it's not love.*

"If it doesn't hurt, it's not love and life without love is merely existing"

And by hurting, I don't mean all the sleepless nights abusing each other, crying because of each other and thinking why the hell I'm in this relationship. By being hurt, I don't mean criticizing each and every thing about your partner and holding the grudges so that you can use them in your next fight, I don't mean avoiding the arguments and arriving at conclusion with an "I will show him/her" statement in mind.

What hurts is what we care. Have you ever cried for those thousands of people who die daily or the lakhs of people who get wounded now and then somewhere across the world, the answer will be "No!! We never ever gave them even a single thought"

But when it comes to people we care and people we love even a slight scratch on their hand can make our eyes wet.We never get sad when some unknown break our heart or trust, but we get sad when the known and loved ones do so. Based on that there are two personalities.

Pessimist:

He/she is the one who always think that "he/she don't love me neither he cares for me, nor that's the reason why he is scolding me and getting angry on me" they think that it is the fault of the second person that their mood is always bad and they are always angry. Such people don't see the bright side and are simply not meant to be in a relationship of love.

Optimist:

These people always look for the positive side.

When they get angry on someone they know that the person in their front is the one they love that's why they are hurt. They know it well that if it is for some other person that it wouldn't have mattered that much.

They know when the second person gets hurt because of them and is angry with them that "*Anger is the most childish way of expressing care*" they know it well that they mean something forthat person. That is the reason he was angry or worried about them. They know that the person loves them and hence he/she is keeping expectation from them and the failure of expectation fulfillment is the reason of their unhappiness

This is called as maturity and the positive instinct. Such thinking boost up the desire and capability to hold the relation strong and long enough and makes one realize about their responsibilities and fault, encourages one to lift himself up and change for the better personality.

*"**Every heart** sings a song, incomplete, until another heart whispers back. Those who **wish** to sing always find **a** song. At the touch of a **lover**,everyone becomes a poet."*

The one who has experienced all this and can feel it with his girl is probably one of the luckiest guy. She is a privilege you got. Respect her for so much she gives you.

Because once she gets attached, she is loyal, she is committed, she is honest, she is faithful, she is dependable, she is caring, she owes herself to you, and she gives you right over her. But there is also something that comes with it. She's jealous, she's clingy, she is annoying, she is over protective, she's emotional, she will fight you like your wife, and she is crazy. You could push her away, but she will never let go, you could piss her off.

But she will never be mad at you, she will smile at your smile, she will celebrate your slightest achievement like crazy, she will always be there for you, you could lie to her, but she still can't stop trusting you, you could keep making mistakes, but she will forgive you over and over, you could make her hate you but she will love you anyway, she will always fall in love with you again and again, but dude don't take this for granted because once she is going to trust you, you are going to feel it.

But *LOL* this is only the positive side friend. You better understand that this stuff doesn't end here. As mentioned in the topic the word *weird* starts to get its meaning from here in the completely different direction.

Remember the face you saw in the crowd and started smiling silently, remember the time when it was only the girl who didn't know about your feelings but the whole world did. The time when everyone in your friend circle is interested in your love story morethan you. It all makes a man feel somewhat differently happy, some out of the world feeling it is. But the surprising aspect of this is that, you are afraid to tell these feelings to that person only for who you are grinding the grains for so long. Confessing this to her is the hardest thing a boy can ever face on the face of earth.

"Getting habitual to her so much that you can't think anything else but her all the time and one day she leaves. It is suddenly an existence crisis. It is painful. Everything feels worthless and the only thing that can save your mental state are some more moments with her. But you can't get them. And the cycle of pain continues to grow bigger and so the love"

When you are away from her, and a time comes when you start forgetting her and enjoying with your friend, when you smile, with a smile comes her one memory that strikes your mind and force you to think "Am I smiling!!?, How?, I'm without her, she's no longer with me, how I forgot her and how can I be happy without her"

But here you need to learn that

"Sometimes the person you want the most is the person you are better without"

1) If she says NO:

   It starts with a heartbreak, a lot of efforts to overcome it, in some cases trying to avoid her so that the "out of sight is out of mind" thing can work. Some try to find a substitute. Some can't let the pain hide. But in the end *the time heals everything.*

2) You can't let her leave:

   Sometimes it seriously gets hard to let the one go this easy that you used to be crazy about. It's hard to see yourself in the mirror without that one person with whom you decided to enjoy the rest of your life. In some cases you can't see the person is happy without you.

3) You don't want to accept the truth:

   After witnessing so much and after a clear rejection from that person, you are still not willing to accept the fact that the person can't be yours and you need to move on. No matter how many times you realize the fact, it got a default reply from your server not to accept it.

4) You still try the same thing:

You keep being optimistic and you look for the chances that the person will come back to you. You feel that she will forget everything. You still can't lose your feelings for her and try to talk to her every time with a new hope. And you are not wrong. If she loves you. Then *only SHE* can stay.

5) You get hurt. Still manages again:

When you talk again, you try being good, forgetting all that happened in the past. Thinking it's a time where you both can change and afresh or at the other side you thinks, let's not talk and let the person go

6) You want to stop, but some forces still make you talk to her. And you lower yourself in your eyes:

The worst thing that happens here in loving the person who doesn't love you back is losing yourself in the process of loving that person so much that you forget that you are special too.

"Sometimes you need to ***forget*** *and* ***forgive*** *some people, but when those people are the same whom you want the most, it becomes the hardest part."*

"Sorry tummy for all the
butterflies Sorry pillow for all
the tears
Sorry heart for
the damage sorry brain you
were right"

One of my friends told me that at this stage you feel being in love is like as if there is a button in front of you which says-*press here* for free candies. But when you actually press that all you get is a bird which shits on your head, but you keep pressing because you are looking at the candy, let's call it the positive side here. And then once in every 100 times you get a candy, and you are like "hurray!! I got the candy" you are encouraged and starts pressing the button again and taking shit all over you.

But every time you get a candy after shit, its d best candy you ever had, like after a slot of bad times, every single happy moment seems precious.

But while you are eating it you will willingly get shit on 99 times in hopes of getting another candy, for a small time of happiness you keep on striving through bad situations again and again and gets yourself broken.But moreover this, one day the candies stop coming. There remain no more positive sides to entertain you just the regret of the past.

You miss the taste of the candy, tries to get back to earn one, but now starts fearing the 99 time shit scene.And over the period of time you stop liking candies

"You can be the sweetest and ripest peach in the world, but still there will be some people who hate peaches"

This clearly means tells us that if you keep yourself in company of toxic people, you slowly stops believing in the healthier ones, about which.

Bob Marley says

"The truth is that everyone in this world is going to hurt you, but it's you who have to decide what matters the most, the pain or the person"

The time when you start giving so much importance to someone or some situation that it don't work anymore the proper way. Thinking too much is really such a pain... when you are with that person everything feels beautiful. You feel like having a reason for every happiness you have, but when you are not with them sometimes during the happy situation you feel like you have moved on but sometimes while having fun enjoying the moments while looking at the smiling and cheerful faces around you, you suddenly realize that you are not with that person and everything every happiness around is fake and can never be completely fruitful without that person.

Wanting to text someone and dying to tell them how you feel type it all, with all the emotions you got inside you and when you are about the press that send button the other side of your somewhere deep inside gives a call and you start feeling way to text and why to start it all over again, you get confused why you get ready to be hurt each time after you fall and your fingers automatically move to backspace erasing all the feelings you just entered and not to send anything at all and just let it go.

Love and madness, I say are no different terms. Once you get into it there is no way out. You just keep falling down for more and more. As the joker said in batman- the movie

"Madness is just like gravity, all you need is just a little push!"

Same is here for love. Once the spark is ignited it burns you completely. Once you happen to fall in love, nothing can control you. It either makes you live with that person or makes you leave that person and consequently yourself too.

What I feel and experienced is

"One **simply** *cannot play* **Love,** *not even from a safe distance, you will definitely fall a victim to it"*

Practicing love is yet another thing. There is no emotion like fake love. Love is just beyond all this. Love is that wonderful feeling you can never imitate. When trying to fool others with fake signs of love and emotions, a man generally ends up fooling himself. He either himself falls in love or can never perform.

*"***One** *can act falling in* **love,** *but one cannot act staying out of it"*

What actually matters is to be in it. One man who thinks just for himself, who is selfish, who sees his own profit when starts caring for someone more than him, when start taking care of someone more than for himself, when his happiness is in the happiness of someone, it isn't less than a miracle, is it? As I said earlier, it's the most selfless act ever created by god, by man, by you or by me it don't matter. Yes indeed, it's a miracle.

"And still, after all this time, the Sun has never said to the Earth,

'You owe me.'

Look what happens with a love like that.

It lights up the sky."

-Hafez

"Only once in your life, I truly believe, you find someone who can completely turn your world around. You tell them things that you've never shared with another soul and they absorb everything you say and actually want to hear more. You share hopes for the future, dreams that will never come true, goals that were never achieved and the many disappointments life has thrown at you. When something wonderful happens, you can't wait to tell them about it, knowing they will share in your excitement.

They are not embarrassed to cry with you when you are hurting or laugh with you when you make a fool of yourself. Never do they hurt your feelings or make you feel like you are not good enough, but rather they build you up and show you the things about yourself that make you special and even beautiful. There is never any pressure, jealousy or competition, but only a quiet calmness when they are around. You can be yourself and not worry about what they will think of you because they love you for who you are.

The things that seem insignificant to most people such as a note, song or walk become invaluable treasures kept safe in your heart to cherish forever. Memories of your childhood come back and are so clear and vivid it's like being young again. Colors seem brighter and more brilliant. Laughter seems part of daily life where before it was infrequent or didn't exist at all. A phone call or two during the day helps to get you through a long day's work and always brings a smile to your face.

In their presence, there's no need for continuous conversation, but you find you're quite content in just having them nearby. Things that never interested you before become fascinating because you know they are important to this person who is so special to you. You think of this person on every occasion and in everything you do.

Simple things bring them to mind like a pale blue sky, gentle wind or even a storm cloud on the horizon. You open your heart knowing that there's a chance it may be broken one day and in opening your heart, you experience a love and joy that you never dreamed possible. You find that being vulnerable is the only way to allow your heart to feel true pleasure that's so real it scares you.

You find strength in knowing you have a true friend and possibly a soulmate that will remain loyal to the end. Life seems completely different, exciting and worthwhile. Your only hope and security is in knowing that they are a part of your life."- Bob Marley

A real relation is one where...

It's as simple as starting with a "Hi" to end nowhere, it may start so unusually so unexpectedly and can last for a lifetime. It's just about the wavelength that needs to be matched, catch and preserved.

A real relationship is where there are no hidden secrets, even if a relationship is to be a secret you shouldn't be in it. You love her, why are you shy to hold her hand in the crowd, stand by her side, have her back. If you love her you can take a stand for her, proud to have her.

It's not about a lip kiss, it's about a kiss on the forehead, it's about getting a hug when you need it most, it's of course about arguments, fights crying and tears, but it's more about supporting each other when going through these stages, because it's about crying for them and being that good that they cry for you. It's about that one good feeling when you see *people crying for you* but the act of shame is to see *people crying because of you.*

"It's when you are close to each other like the waterdrops are to clouds, like the lyrics are to the lips, like the kajal is to the eyes, the way secret is to heart, like fragrance is to breathe, like lover is to arms, dreams is to vision, like child is to mother and waves are to sea."

Though it includes sitting on the bike so close that even air can't pass, but it's also about that sweet walks on the road where you buy balloons for her, where you make every flower feel her presence where you both enjoy the roadside Bhel (Indian snack) along with the funky attires and masks the uncle is selling along the road, where you both enjoy teasing the people on the road, doing some crazy shit.

It's when you are waiting for her in the cinema hall and she don't arrive, and you can concentrate on the movie ,the glamorous actress just keeps navigating across the complete theatre, turns 90 degrees every other second, you are restless because your princess hasn't arrived yet.

It's about pushing each other away with fun and pulling close to each other with that much love and affection. It's not about you over her or her over you, it's about your head on her lap or hers on your shoulder. It's less about " Do whatever you want, I don't care" or " You should do what I told you to" it's more about " Dear you should think it over again" it's not about letting the problems go and avoiding them by not talking. It's about facing them and trying to solve without harsh feeling.

A real relationship is where, when she asks you that whether you love her or not and you reply NO! And she knows you are lying. You say you hate her in such tone where she punch you with love, *hugs you and say 'you liar... I love you too'*

Love is when you both are talking at 3 am and she says I am sleepy and you reply "ok, no problem, lets sleep" and she warns you not to dare to cut the phone and starts talking afresh because none of you wants to sleep now and why will you since the reality is much more interesting and pleasant than your dreams when you both make each one feel so special. It makes you confident, even when the whole world is against you, because you are confident and believe that you can even fight the whole world with one hand when she is holding another.

That time it doesn't matter who are on your side and who are not, it doesn't matter where there are people who like you or are there any people who think good of you, treat you as an idol, trust you or believe you. It doesn't matter what the outside world thinks about you, what matters is what she thinks for you, because that time she is your world and which is far bigger and more meaningful.Love is when in her arms lies your destiny, in her wish lies your wish, When her actions tell your story, When her heartbeat is a fuel your's."

"Sometimes the road to ***happinessis*** *so narrow that you both cannot walk* ***together*** *through, that time there remains only one option, either you leave each other and run for the glory road or you both become one."*

When you see her it's like

Like the Blossoming rose,

Like the Rays of hope.

Like a deer in the forest,
Like an athlete full of zest.
Like a lamp in the temple,
Like a life feeling ample.
Like the feel of the dawn,
Like the grace of the swan.
Like the melody of the sitar,
Like the rage of the guitar.
Like a flight of angels in the sky,
Like the pot that makes you high.
Like the beauty of peacock's dance,
Like the feel of sheer romance.
Like the completeness of the silent talk,
Like the wine from the Medoc.
Like the colors of the life,
Life the music of the fife.
Like the calmness of the wind,
Like the beauty of the hind.

Though there are many forms of relationships and love that surrounds you each one of them have a different perspective, a different meaning a different reason and of course a different name and significance. A study suggests that,

If you love someone just because they look gorgeous then it's not actually love, it is "***infatuation***"

If you love someone and are just sticking to them not because you want to be with them that so much, but because others think that you should not leave them then its again not love, it's simply a "***compromise***"

If you are with someone because you cannot forget their touch and are just obsessed with it then its "***lust***" but not love.

If you are with someone because you have been kissed by them and so you cannot leave them, then it's not love again, it's "***inferiority complex***"

If you are in a relationship with someone thinking that it would hurt them if you leave them, then it's not a big thing, but a "***charity***"

If you share everything with someone and misunderstood it as love then you must know that it's just a "***friendship***" but not

Love. Just sharing everything don't make you love birds.But the real love is when you and the other person counts as one and you feel pain for the other person more than he/she feels for them.

When you cry for them when they are unstable. If you stay with them no matter what. If you let them go, knowing that theyhave to go but he/she doesn't want to think that attachment and that understanding is what is called love and real relationship.

'People think a soulmate is your perfect fit, and that's what everyone wants. But a true soulmate is a mirror, the person who shows you everything that is holding you back, the person who brings you to your own attention so you can change your life.

A true soulmate is probably the most important person you'll ever meet, because they tear down your walls and smack you awake. But to live with a soul mate forever? Naah! Too painful. Soulmates, they come into your life just to reveal another layer of yourself to you, and then leave.

A soulmates purpose is to shake you up, tear apart your ego a little bit, show you your obstacles and addictions, break your heart open so new light can get in, make you so desperate and out of control that you have to transform your life, then introduce you to your spiritual master."

– Elizabeth Gilbert, *Eat, Pray, Love*

Love should not be the call given to lust by lust. Because

"Since sex got easier to get love got harder to find"

While forming a new relationship as the friends say that don't give her too much importance, let her feel your absence, ignore her sometimes, there are various techniques to make her fall in love with you, compliment her friend, make her jealous. Be available for her when she needs you, but not all the time.

These are nothing but strategies that you are using to love someone or to make her fall in love with you. But just think about it, is this a war, a game or something, why you need strategies, why you need to use your brains, why you need techniques. Can't we keep it different from all those acts, stuffs we are facing each and everyday in life, we should treat it as clear as glass and not as those steps and rules and regulations we have to learn to survive the daily life.

It should be clean and clear. A perfect relationship is where the love just flows without a dam, without an obstacle, where you don't have to use your mind, where the heart does the complete job, when we achieve that status in a certain relationship then that relations get strengthen with those threads of affection that can never be broken.

"Love is when the guy stops thinking about sex and the girl starts thinking about it"

A relationship is not a compromise, not an adjustment, not an act performed to meet one's need to survive and to take name of the family ahead, a relationship doesn't demand just support for self-purpose, and is not established on such single need, a real relationship is not where the boy and girl come together because girls need support to live to handle them and serve the family and boys need a girl to mate, extend their family and take care of infants.

What I came across since last few years is that the number of girls has decreased and literally there are no girls available for marriage. Hence the girls are demanding more and more. They demand single child where there should be no restriction of his mom and dad, they should live separately, and when tried to understand the reason behind such type of behavior of girls, one can come to know that since even the girls nowadays are earning 2-3 lakhs a month why should they listen to anyone!!?? What!!? Is it a compromise to marriage otherwise!? Are you marrying just for the need!!? Is it what it is meant to be?? Of course not. It is an attachment, connection between hearts, as said by anonymous, the couples are made in heaven.

This is not the way it should be. One must understand the delicateness, the purity of this relation, I agree that nowadays it has become a need to marry. But marrying for self-benefit, money or related is never going to work out. We won't be any different from those animals in the jungle which mate so they can keep their breed going. We got emotions, we must feel ourselves lucky that we are bestowed by one of the most self-less act-love of God.

The next time you start adoring someone or someone started loving you remember Forms of love/respect can be many. There are people who fall for some or the other. There are various reasons attached always, you believe or not, accept or not, but falling in love is not always the way they say in book. All have their own reasons.

The success of the other person, this form implies when you start liking someone for the success they are achieving and the hill they have climbed in the society on the basis of their capabilities, luck or whatever.

The fame of the person:

When the person is famous, loved and adored all over, you start getting attracted towards him automatically, when everyone is praising someone, when everyone hates someone, and you are living in the same atmosphere, you become one of those.It's similar to Facebook. Where everyone who joins Facebook starts loving Eminent and Hating Justin Bieber and no one knows why?!!

The money:

The money is yet another factor which seems to set the desire of having someone on fire. The money attracts you or the person is not the matter, you get the person you get the money, you get the money you may not need the person. The money seems to disguise prosperity, good status, stable life and may attract people and push them to fall in love.

The charm:

Charm is on the inside, it's the positive energy you give out when you stand, you sit, talk, run, walk just everytime and there is not bound to it, you don't bath for a week, it's still going to be there, you are not rich it's still going to be there.

But the thing is success, status and money makes everyone look charming. Is it for real or not that is yet another question?

Personality:

A personality, way of behavior, the way you treat everyone, the gentleman in you can also attract crowds no doubt. And may be the one who falls in love with your charm and personality and the kind of person you are, are considered to be the real lovers.

Now the question that arises is,

They say when someone respect someone for money, the respect or love is not true, it's not for the person but for the money. But ever wondered who earned thatmoney and on whose ability?? The person itself, right? Then isn't people are falling in love with the ability of that person.

They say using money to achieve something and thinking something of yourself if you have money is a bad attitude, but here again, the man had earned all that for himself with the help of his skills, mastery then isn't all this a part of himself only. Doesn't he has right to do so?

Same case applies to when someone is famous, reputed, and successful!! He achieved all that so he has the right to use all of it.

People say she or he loves your money and not you!! What type of question is this!! She will leave you when your money vanishes, he will leave you if you won't be beautiful.

Love at first sight they say, how can you know about someone and their personality if you never meet them? Before you fall in love with the way they look or the area they are surrounded by, you may fall in love with the way you see them interacting with others. But is it love?

They say, only those people stay who loves you for you and not all those things that are mentioned above. Can anyone explain what is meant by loving me for being me? It basically must mean that they love me for my personality, or my behavior towards them, or for being nice. Isn't this also a type of being materialistic like above cases? They are going to leave me if I change my behavior, if I am not kind any more or if I lose my charm.

Everything everyone is there for a reason, it may be money, success, fame or your kindness, and you lose something, Bamm!! They are gone

Those who are going to stay will stay forever, no matter you lose your status, your iconic style, your behavior towards them, are they fools to stay even if you can't give them anything kindness or love or stable living!! No, they are absolutely not!! They are not fools!!They are themselves good!! Good is in them, if they loved you for your status and fame, it is not necessary that they will leave when you lose, they help you achieve it again, and that's love or respect! **That's careless!! And that's complicated!!**

What happens when you suddenly fall in love with your best friend?

So you started to feel something for your best friend, and even you don't know how out of nowhere you have encountered this feeling, you need to relax because you are going to face a really hard time, maybe with chances of success or even failure, but what you must know is if this work out you are going to be the luckiest person I assure, because even studies shows that when you marry best friend, the rate of success is maximized, but the sweeter it sounds the harder it is.

If a day or two had already passed and you can't stop thinking about her, buddy!! You are screwed. !! You may get friendzoned, dumbed or you may get lucky. Haha!! Nothing less than a Bollywood climax, isn't it?

We are besties!! What can be the problem??Must be the question in your mind. I would say "That is the problem", what are you going to tell her. Suppose you are friends from over a decade and you tell her that you started liking her, maybe she will laugh you out. And I am sure even we get confused what is this happening to us.

You want to stick around with her, you like her company, you want to be with her 24x7. You like it when the way you both laugh together and tease the hell out of everyone, you will love to hang out with each other, and you get mad even at her smile.

"If you live to be a hundred, I want to live to be a hundred minus one day so I never have to live without you."- A.A. Milne, Winnie-the-Pooh

Maybe she know this and that's why you guys are best friends. And you don't need to express that and you are neither supposed to. But what when you suddenly want to make her realize how important she is to you! When you want her to know that she is the best thing ever happened to you, how you are going to tell her all this? And even if you do, won't it be awkward it for you and her.

It will be really confusing for her and you to believe in what's going on. More than 10 years have passed and both of you never had felt anything like that for each other and why suddenly then. Is this an attraction?? But if this is an attraction why it didn't happen before in so many years? Why suddenly. Maybe because this is what it is destined for. This is not a sudden urge of love, it may be that you never realized it for yourself. Maybe you were too immature for it or maybe you don't wanted to accept It before or maybe that was the age of friendship when you went through all this, and moreover for the same reason it is called as 'falling in love', because you never realize when it is going to happen, it just happens.

Telling her about your feelings is the hardest part, first you have to make yourself sure and after that you think "What she will think? What If she will take the wrong meaning? I didn't become her friend for this reason, you even start doubting your character that how can you feel so for someone who was purely your friend? What if she says no? Can I continue to be friend with her? Can I even make eye contact with her, that's going to hurt so much?

But if you are sure you really started loving her, you should not let her go, because she is the one who is going to turn your world around and bring the best out of it. She is the one who understand you better than anyone else and knows your moods, happiness and sadness. And only she can as a friend can kick your ass at the right times to bring you on the right path and no one else can. Only lucky ones have the privilege to have soul mate and best friend as the same person.

Commitments:

Commitment and relationships teach a lot to man. Some relationships try to teach that don't care about people and let the 'feeling good about them' attitude go to hell, some part of relation teach you that why man is a man why emotions matter and why the world is so beautiful. Some relations bring s you to the stage of complications where deciding whether to let every-thing go or whether to stay without knowing the complete truth as if you are standing behind the curtain directing your own movie of life, while some relation gives you the courage, makes up your mind, awaken your heart and make you realize that some things are not for letting them go, some emotions memories makes you strong enough to face the truth accept the reality, gives the courage to let everything happened in the past to be buried deep inside and never to be dig out. They teach you that it is never too late to start a new beginning when both people care about each other .some part of the relation makes you strong enough to fight all the odds, some teaches to be desperate, some teaches patience, some teaches you hope, some shows the dying expectations, some teaches that listening is more important than expressing.

Learn that *there are always three part of story 1.your's, 2. their's, 3.the truth.* Some teaches that time heals everything while some makes you realize that many things gets worse with the time. Some makes you feel happy, some makes you feel sad, some makes you learn, some makes you burn, every relation is to be earn. that over-whelming happiness of being with some person, that soul drying sadness of getting hurt, that silence of being ignored, that pride of being cared. There is so much to feel, so much to learn but the important is to respect them and give the proper treatment that our lives deserve, that is enjoy them. These are the emotions that make us human.

They teach that no man can enjoy being bad and hard to others, sometimes it's their heart that has being broken or the expectations that has shattered or the feelings that were killed which make them what they are with you, with others

They teach that two people care about each other and can expect exactly different things from each other. They teach that it is always better to express your love and state your anger and not vice versa.

Sometimes the thinking don't match, expectations are not fulfilled but it doesn't mean that relation won't survive, some things are need to be left back forgotten replaced with new ones that suit's both. Free yourself from negative peopleSpend time with nice people who are smart, driven and likeminded, relationships should help you and not hurt you.

Surround yourself with people who reflect the person you want to be and will encourage you in every aspect of life. Choose friends who are proud to know you, people who feels lucky of themselves for having you, people who admire you, love to spend time with you, who makes your day little brighter no matter whether they do something or not, it's just their presence that makes everything works. Life is too short to spend time with people who are always worried and criticizing life; such people suck happiness out of you leaving you as skeleton filled with sadness, regrets and bones of worthless thoughts. Such people suck the happiness out of you. When you free yourself from such people, you free yourself to be you and being truly you is the only true way to live

The biggest gift you can give yourself is being you without hurting anyone and being kind to all. Having some special day waiting for it being desperate and scared and it ending up not the way you wanted.No special day. Celebrate, buy cake, and blow balloons everyday.

SOCIETY AND YOU

"Society, be a part of it and not apart from it"

Yes, we are a part of society and should behave accordingly, but always remember that it is the same society that says abortion is wrong and then talks about teenage abortion, it is the same society that sells products that guarantees natural ingredients, good looks, perfect hair, smooth skin, flawless tone and uses models on their box who is half photoshopped, with fake eyelashes, tons of makeup It's the same society where the leaders talk about social service, social worker talks about self-service and end up just serving self. The society where priests talk about donation, who taught money is not everything and own so much that you will fail to count in a lifetime. Parents who want well educated children, but wonder and marvel how rich Richard Branson is.

Governments that speak about peace, but endorse war to bring the same. They say they believe in education and higher learning and this is the only way a nation can progress, and then why they increase the tuition fees every year, don't they run a business. We are the generation who don't need to search a whole lot of books to get what they are looking for, they simply Google it, we are the generation who have imagination far much broader than those in the last century, but we are also that generation where teachers reject the best innovations, best articles, concepts because they are not presented according to the rule book, because the language is informal.

Your future is not a result of these trends in the society unless you endure a caliber to change the world around you so much better that others can blindly follow it.

Story

Once a group of 50 people was attending a seminar. Suddenly the speaker stopped and started giving each one aballoon. Each one was asked to write his/her name on it using a marker pen. Then all the balloons were collected and put in another room.

Now these delegates were left in that room and asked to find the balloon which had their name written, within 5 minutes. Everyone was frantically searching for their name, colliding with each other, pushing around others and there was utter chaos.

At the end of 5 minutes no one could find their own balloon. Now each one was asked to randomly collect a balloon and give it to the person whose name was written on it. Within minutes everyone had their own balloon. The speaker began exactly this is happening in our lives. Everyone is frantically looking for happiness all around, not knowing where it is. Our happiness lies in the happiness of other people. Give them their happiness; you will get your own happiness. And this is the purpose of human life.

No matter how true you say, till the time you don't have a status no one going to trust you

"Learn to show your respect to people when they are alive and not when they are gone."

How to earn respect for yourself?

The one important quality you need to prove yourself among the people is a Showmanship and a great *oratory skills.*

Making people believe what you want is in their interests is real art.

"Being diplomatic is that godly capability where you tell the people to go to hell and the people simply look forward for the journey"

But also remember that "No matter what you are, no matter where you stand, the one time you express or made someone realize that you need them, Bamm!! It's *over. The status, the respect that very position of yours is all lost. Suddenly they start looking down at you.*

"Dependency is a curse"

Same thing happen when you make people feel precious. They start acting pricey.

You achieve it when the one who loves you supports you against the one whom you are not actually against.

Example - Sachin Tendulkar and Ricky Pointing are actually good friends but their fans try to prove either of them superior.

"You don't need a special recognition from society, nor a dignity award because they all feel small in front of the proud you feel when your dad tells his wife how much he is proud of his son"

You see the world the way you treat it even if it's not that way.Suppose when you are cheating on someone or are doing wrong with someone the moment when you are at their place you start thinking that the person is also cheating on you and doing something wrong with you "Why will he treat me properly when I didn't?"

Story:

An economics professor at a local college made a statement that he had never failed a single student before, but had recently failed an entire class. That class had insisted that Obama's socialism worked and that no one would be poor and no one would be rich, a great equalizer. The professor then said, "OK, we will have an experiment in this class on Obama's plan". All grades will be averaged and everyone will receive the same grade so no one will fail and no one will receive an A.... (Substituting grades for dollars - something closer to home and more readily understood by all).

After the first test, the grades were averaged and everyone got a B. The students who studied hard were upset and the students who studied little were happy. As the second test rolled around, the students who studied little had studied even less and the ones who studied hard decided they wanted a free ride too so they studied little.

The second test average was a THE! No one was happy. When the 3rd test rolled around, the average was an F.

As the tests proceeded, the scores never increased as bickering, blame and name-calling all resulted in hard feelings and no one would study for the benefit of anyone else.

To their great surprise, ALL FAILED and the professor told them that socialism would also ultimately fail because when the reward is great, the effort to succeed is great, but when government takes all the rewards away, no one will try or want to succeed.These are possibly the 5 best sentences you'll ever read and all applicable to this experiment:

1. You cannot legislate the poor into prosperity by legislating the wealthy out of prosperity.
2. *What one person receives without working for, another person must work for without receiving.*
3. *The government cannot give to anybody anything that the government does not first take from somebody else.*
4. *You cannot multiply wealth by dividing it!*
5. *When half of the people get the idea that they do not have to work because the other half is going to take care of them, and when the other half gets the idea that it does no good to work because somebody else is going to get what they work for, that is the beginning of the end of any nation.*

"Don't harm your interest for the sake of loss of others and don't make your loss for the intention that others should not get profit"

How to perform your little duties towards the society? And why should you do it?

I remember one incident during my college days.

It was a time of cultural week and gathering, so our classroom was allotted to the team for practice, so all the benches were displaced and only a few were left which were arranged in improper way. The next day when we entered the class to attain lectures, we kept the arrangement of the benches as it is.

We didn't move a single bench, even for the sake of our convenience, the number of benches was also less, so when students arrived there was no place for them to sit. We all started complaining that college is like that or like this.

We didn't even strive for the sake of our comfort. That time our class teacher told us this is the simple concept which is applicable everywhere, you cannot blame the college (at local level) or the government for all the problems you are facing. You have to sweep your own house. Sometimes the efforts are not for the sake of *yourself, but for others so that they can feel better.*Suppose if a rock is lying in the middle of the road, what are you going to do?

- **Blame game?**

"Whenever you feel like criticizing anyone, always remember that all the people in this world haven't had an advantage that you've had."

- **Stumble upon the rock and curse people for not moving it. But still won't learn?**

"People who don't learn from their history of mistakes are bound to be doomed in the history itself"

- **Avoid it?**

"Closing your eyes doesn't mean that it don't exists and it won't affect you"

- **Move it so others can also walk freely?**

Don't try to change people for yourself or for the society.

"One must take care that while trying to change people, over a course he himself may get changed."

"It is always better to be the change which you want to see in the world."

Now just think for a moment, about the incident mentioned in the above story where we sat without rearranging the benches. Those were us who suffered, those were us who were not able to sit properly. Those were us who blamed. And those were us who were in loss. Neither our teacher had any problem nor our college. They both were doing their jobs and earning their money. In such cases we should change our stubborn attitude. We should learn that charity begins at home and change starts with self.

Let us consider second case where the stone is lying on the road. It may be you or your relatives who will stumble upon the rock. The next time you have to take that road you may hit it or even your relatives. Those who are reluctant to stand up against the wrong are as guilty as the person committing it.

Remember,

'The darkest place in the hell are reserved for those who maintain their state of neutrality at the time of crisis"-Paulo Coelho

Have you ever wondered why a human life cost so much as compared to our animal counterparts??

Ever wondered why a chicken life costs just a 100 ₹ while a goat cost some thousand bucks and horse may cost some lakhs?

This is a simple example to make us understand how society works.

A chicken is useful just for one time, once you eat it, its work is done, a goat provides you with milk for years and you can even use it for meat. And last one the horse, it is a symbol of royalty and can even you can even earn you millions.

Ok, now let's study each one of them.

One common thing these both share is a lack of expression of emotions. A chicken can't express anything, a goat may dosometimes, but the horse is above them both in case of emotions as it can express love, care and even gratitude towards its master.

So by now I think it must be getting clearer to you that your importance and your value (not cost) increases by how much you contribute to the society, and not only this but also on how much you express yourself.

Just think for a while, will anyone sell a chicken, which can express itself for just 100 bucks, or will anyone among you will respect people who don't contribute to the society or hardly express themselves.

The same law applies everywhere, you are valuable and important to others only if you can do something. No one in the world is going to entertain useless living beings except you are a cute little kitten, which certainly you are not, and even cats are expected to catch the mice for the free milk and love they get.

No matter what you are capable of or what are your skills, but if you can't use them for the society that developed you, you are not going places.

And if you won't express yourself, you may eventually find yourself getting slaughtered with knives of life's conditions, or running races against yourself.

Here is one corporate lesson that teaches the importance of **the way of expression and demanding**

Jack and Max are walking to the church for the Sunday prayer. Jack wonders whether it would be all right to smoke while

Praying.

Max replies, "Why don't you ask the Priest?" So Jack goes up to the Priest and asks, "Father, may I smoke while I pray?" The Priest replies, "No, my son, you may not! That's utter disrespect to our religion." Jack goes back to his friend and tells him what the good Priest told him.

Max says, "I'm not surprised. You asked the wrong question. Let me try."

And so Max goes up to the Priest and asks, "Father, may I pray while I smoke?" To which the Priest eagerly replies, "By all means, my son. By all means. You can always pray whenever you want to."

Moral of the story:

The approval you want depends on the way you ask for it!!

Our society is little difficult for those who are between the age 22 to 27.

Your ex- BFs & GFs are getting married, Your Career has just started, Elders treat you as unproven theorems, and teenagers feel that you are too old to have in their groups. You seem to enjoy both cartoon and news. You can no longer eat whatever you wish without putting on weight. You are not invited for weekend cricket/- football matches. Every Aunt you meet asks 'When are you getting married' while uncle asks 'What have you thought about your career'

When the reality is that you are just riding the wave and going with the flow. You have all the confidence in the world, but little achievements to show, you already have the first-hand experience of the life, you know that whatever you have been taught about the world in schools has been sheer waste of time. You can be denied of a job even after passing the test and you could be given a job if you know someone placed high enough.

Politics till now was a dirty word, but now you feel it everywhere. You know now love is not that blind and that friendship has its terms and conditions. You know there is nothing for granted and free lunches are not free. Your over-confidence is now making way for a humble conscience. You now know it is not exactly what we thought it would be. (Internet)

How people around us affect us?

We learn many things from the society when we start seeing the brighter side in the people.

The time you spend with people around you, with the one you like the one you love and the one you care can teach you a lot more than any school or instituteout there in the world. But there is contradiction in what we learn and it differs from person to person. If you don't have a stable mind (somewhat like me) you can be confused because for some time of life you will find yourself on one shore and meanwhile you can find your other leg across another shore.

When you are living happily with those people, you think "Wow Man!! The world is such a beautiful place. Why the hell I never realized it before? I am going to enjoy each and every moment with those I love. Memories are great assets to treasure.

When you get hurt, you think "The world is such a mean place, are relationships meant to be hurt, is care meant to be hurt". You want to go away from them. But you can't.

I don't know what makes you stop from being away from the people who hurt you each time, is it the love for them? Or is it the care? Or it is just the desperation? Or the habit you have about them? Whether you don't like to end relations with the one who gave you so much to remember or it is that you just think too much.

"When the level of your caring goes to infinity, to zero lands your dignity"

You try to forget and forgive people. But when you try to forget all those bad things that has happened with you, when you suddenly recall some memories you shared with those people, when you suddenly encounter them, a deep feeling shoots through your heart recalling each and every good time you spend with them. It makes you feel how lonely and alone you are without those people and how badly you need them. But now the real problem arises, because can you step back? NO!! You decided already not to look back, to be stubborn and not to be attached, you decided to move on. You got a little ego or maybe you are afraid to be hurt again. You try to be hard on the inside, but for some people, it's not simply possible, in fact it gets harder with time, it gets hard when you have seen so much of these things.

You are now living two lives. One which wants to recollect all those lost memories and the other which is not strong enough to get back to that battlefield of emotions. Either you are too strong to live by yourself without those who once made your life worth living and taught you the true meaning of living.

But remember

"If your loved ones are your weakness, then you are the strongest person in the world"

There are various types of people in the world. Let's take a look at them as we sort them in various categories.

Which one are you?

(Introspect the type of person you are, and which you one want to be, write it down if necessary which one you think you should be like)

Category One

1) Who feels there will be nothing left at the end so why not to enjoy now?
2) There are those who feel that what's the use to enjoy when nothing is going to remain in the end
3) There are those who free themselves from all wants and desires because they know nothing remains in the end.

Category Two

It is said that there are two types of people

1) The one who lives in the spotlight
2) The one who pays to see such people

But I believe that there's a third one too. Those people who organize shows of those in the 1st category for those in the 2nd category, so to earn money from them.

Category Three

One man was using a brand new iPhone 5 gifted to him by his uncle

- 1st man says I wish I had an iPhone like that.
- 2nd man says you rather wish you had an uncle like him.
- 3rd man says I wish I could be an uncle like that.

The mentioned three types of people depicts the three types of personalities, vision, attitudes.

No doubt the 3rd man is the most mature and sophisticated one.

Let us consider that all the wishes of each one of them is fulfilled. So what will they be having now?

1st man will only have an iPhone

2nd man will have an iPhone and a rich family with big heart.

3rd man will himself be so rich. He will be having a big heart. He will be the person who gifted that iPhone, we will own respect, love from not only society but from his family too. He will have self-satisfaction.

Category Four

There are again two types of people

1) Those people who, after seeing something bad or unethical to try to stop it and prevent it from happening no matter what.
2) Those people who just see, feel bad and do nothing
3) Those people who study those cases, observe them, add them to their experience book so that they can use it to learn the principles of life and never expose that they know it so that people don't stop carrying those activities in front of them.

Category Five

The other three types of people

1) One who believes that Hindu, Muslim unity should be encouraged.
2) The one who thinks that encouraging Hindu-Muslim unity is a work we got our tails tied to, if both communities are good enough then no need to take such campaigns.
3) Those who thinks that giving a speech on Hindu Muslim unity can make them earn.

I remember a story which gives beautiful and easy lessons by describing the types of people around us.

There was this robbery in Guangzhou, the robber shouted to everyone: "All don't move, money belongs to the state, life belongs to you". Everyone in the bank laid down quietly.

This is called ***"Mind Changing Concept —>Changing the conventional way of thinking".***

One lady lay on the table provocatively, the robber shouted at her "Please be civilized! This is robbery and not a rape!"

This is called ***"Being Professional —> Focus only on what you are trained to do!"***

When the robbers got back, the younger robber (MBA trained) told the older robber (who is only primary school educated),

"Big bro, let's count how much we got", the older robber rebutted and said,

"You very stupid, so much money, how to count, tonight TV will tell us how much we robbed from the bank!"

This is called ***"Experience —> nowadays experience is more important than paper qualifications!"***

After the robbers left, the bank manager told the bank supervisor to call the police quickly.

The supervisor says "Wait, wait, wait, let's put the 5 million RMB *we embezzled into the amount the robbers robbed".*

*This is called "***Swim with the tide —> converting an unfavorable situation to your advantage!"**

The supervisor says "It will be good if there is a robbery every month". This is called ***"Killing Boredom —> Happiness is most important."***

The next day, TV news reported that 100 million RMB *was taken from the bank. The robbers counted and counted and counted, but they could only count 20 million* RMB.

The robbers were very angry and complained "We risked our lives and only took 20 million RMB*, the bank manager took 80Million* RMB *with a snap of his fingers. It looks like it is better to be educated to be a thief!"*

This is called ***"Knowledge is worth as much as gold!"***

The bank manager was smiling and happy because his loss on the CINOPEC shares is now covered by this robbery.

This is called ***"Seizing the opportunity"*** *—> daring to take risks"*

The good people.

These are the happy people who live minimally, tell the truth, never make excuses, take time to listen, don't hold grudges, choose friends wisely, always talk good of others, establish personal control, dream big, see problems as challenges, nurture social relationships, avoid social comparisons, treat everyone with kindness, exercise, don't sweat the small stuff, accept what cannot be changed avoid seeking approval from others, express gratitude for they already have, eat well, wake up at the same time every morning and get absorbed in the now"

There are a lot of good people around us. There are those who appreciate, there are those who care, there are those who feel, there are those for whom people means a lot as much as they mean to others. There are people who take the happiness in seeing the world smile. There are those who before thinking about themselves work hard for others. They wake up so that they can do something for others, they sleep so that they can wake up tomorrow again for the same.

Good people aren't only those who do some or other things for others. Doing something always doesn't matter, sometimes what matter is just being good, just being humans.

Sometimes you don't have to prove what you are and what you do. Sometimes you don't have to tell what you are; that time your acts shows what you are and what you feel. Sometimes just a smile is enough to express it all, there are those who just put a hand around your shoulder, cheer you up, buy you a chocolate these little things means a lot.

"I realized that the best and worst thing about being a good person is being a good person itself"

A Real Life Incident

When I was in second year, our lecture was going on and I was completing some other work during the lecture of our class teacher, and unfortunately or fortunately she caught me?

She took my work and told me to get out of the class, and I was like giving stubborn expression, not changing a single emotion on my face, actually I was feeling guilty about what happened, but from outside I didn't show any guilt since my relation with that teacher was not that good, don't know why, it was just like a cold war, we never argued, but it was just there, she kept my work on her table and I just got up from my place, took my bag and went away without saying even a sorry, I thought she will again get angry on me, she always kept bullying me then why to say sorry, but then I realized that my assignments were with her and so I just ran behind her after the lecture got over, and there it was the most unexpected reply.

When I said sorry to her, she said "you please go, I don't want to see your face" I said ma'am it won't happen next time then she replied "your attitude is very bad and you don't have respect for anyone" and I just stood there for minutes so shocked that how can she say so to me, I was always praised for the respect I give to elders, especially teachers until now. She said that "There was not a single expression of guilt on my face, I was behaving stubborn, I don't have manners and I don't care about righteous."

I learned that time one important lesson that

"Being a good person is like being a goalkeeper, it don't matter how many goals a goalkeeper saves, people only remember the one he misses"

Our society is a weird place. *We don't even know who will cry when we will die? We people make it difficult for ourselves only. It's a place where* if we fail just once, no matter even if it is the first time it can prove to be our last time. Our society gives enough changes to unworthy people to make it up to the mark, but they hardly realize the heart of those few good ones. That is the reason that sometimes the people choose to be bad instead of being good. Maybe because when people notice a deed of goodness from someone who is least expected to do it, it is appreciated in a great way, but on the other hand, when a person who have many expectations clinched to his image, a simple mistake can be fatal. The depth of lowness people will make him feel will be painful.

But at the end of the day the decision of being good or being *not so good* lies in our hands, where the weightage and the advantage of being good always surpasses the other one.

Being a good person is just not being good to others, doing good deeds, giving money to poor, taking down at kitten from a tree, it's when you keep doing your deeds without expecting any outcomes, any appraisals. More than just being good it's about being good along with good attitude.

Maintaining the status you earned is a difficult task. Once you achieve it, the next is the real challenge. Sometimes it just don't matter what you start and what you initiate. Sometimes what matter is how you take it ahead and how you raise it higher? Very often what matters to the people around you is the result and not the path you are on. People sometimes lack the ability to feel the goodness that is inside, due to which they appreciate it only when they can see it. This makes them judgmental about you. But still, be good anyway.

It may sound crazy, but remember

"Only crazy people create history and wise people just read the history and they take out faults in it to prove that they are wise enough".

-Jagdish Joshi

Random Story

When asked to a group of students that whether the oldage homes should increase or decrease in India then all the students replied that the number should increase thinking that older people can accommodate, but the right answer was the number should decrease, which basically means that the number of people who need such homes should decrease which is better than a lot of needy people getting lots of oldage homes.

Some Quotes

'There is no difference between a man in intelligence or race, so profound as the difference between sick and well'

– The Great Gatsby

'I am not afraid of those people who got potential and are doing excellent in their respective field, but am jealous of those who are able with potential and are away from the spotlight."

"Only bad thing about killing bad people is that you can do it only once."

'Be good to others, but don't waste your time proving it."

'Think before you speak, but not so much that you lose your Time of speaking"

"Once you achieve a status in society, no matter what you say, it's always correct and desperately followed".

DEVELOPING THE INSIDE YOU

(Here is a small guide to develop your personality!! What!! A personality development guide!! .NO!! Don't worry, it's not another guide from the market.A very small collection of very basic tips with short stories. No boring lectures in front, I assure.)

Discover Yourself

Have you ever thought what you will be giving the society when you will walk away? Will you have the privilege to see faces crying for you when your soul will be leaving the body with a smile? Discover what your heart is calling for, what your mind is fetching. Clear the thoughts and bring out the changes.

Being Positive:

If you think you can and if you think you can't, in both cases you are right. - Henry Ford

Each day comes with its challenges, but why to be negative when you can be positive.

A positive attitude can bring out miracles

- Increases productivity.
- Fosters teamwork.
- Solves problems.
- Improves quality.

- Makes for congenial atmosphere.
- Breeds loyalty.
- Increase profits.
- Fosters better relationships with employers, employees, and customers.
- Reduces stress.
- Helps a person become a contributing member of society and an asset to their country.
- Makes for a pleasing personality.

Story

What is an Attitude?

One time a student asked his teacher, sir, what is the attitude?

In reply teacher pointed finger to 3 laborers who were making bricks and tell him to ask them what they are doing afterwards you will get the answer of your question

The student got confused and thought why, sir, hasreplied in such a way, but at last he decided to ask that question to 3 of them one by one.

The student went near 1st labor and asked him. Excuse me what you are doing?

He got angry and repllied, "can't you see what I am doing stupid fellow?"

Then student went to 2nd labor and asked him the same question. He replied in a normal way that this work will give some money to him through which he can provide food for his family. Then at last student went to 3rd labor asked him the same question. He looked at the student and gave him a smile and said dear, "I have been given a responsibility of constructing huge buildings and for that my preparation is going on". Finally, the student got his answer.

Moral: - It does not matter what work you are doing rather you must be passionate with your work and must know what contribution you are going give to the country through your work. This is called ATTITUDE. Always look for the higher meaning of your work:

Focus on the worthy:

'The person who tries to do everything ultimately achieves nothing."

'Don't run behind everything; learn to sort out what is important and what should be given the priority

Optimistic Approach:

I heard one story about an interview which I think explain this part completely.

During an interview the interviewer asked a girl candidate what if one morning you woke up and found that you were pregnant? That girl smartly replied- I will be very excited, will take an off to celebrate with my husband. That girl was selected without any further questions. Any normal unmarried girl could have shocked to hear this, but she managed it well, I will say extremely well. She kept calm and let the optimistic approach to guide her. Why should I think it in the wrong way, when I can be positive and be happier, she said when later asked.

This is what an optimistic and positive approach is. It even shows the presence of mind.

One story that teaches us not only optimism but the proper way of thinking.

Once a married couple happens to travel by a bus to some place. The route passes through steep slopes and tall Ghats. Suddenly the man's wife made a plan to pay a visit to her relatives who lives nearby. So she urges her husband to make the conductor stop the bus so that they can get out. After some arguments they came out of the bus and travel to the nearby temple to take blessings before going to relatives place, and what happened next was something they could have never imagined. Rockslide takes place and unfortunately a huge rock falls on the bus just 10mins later they both left the bus in front of their eyes. And there happened to be no survivors.

The wife after seeing such horrible incident screams "Thank God!! We were not in that bus" and the man in a low voice exhales 'I wish we could have been in that bus" the wife asks him "Are you normal!!? What nonsense you are talking" the man replies "if we were in that bus, the bus wouldn't have lagged in time which was wasted while arguing and dropping us and we would have crossed the Ghats before the accident"

Instead of saying "Stop being negative" a real ***optimistic*** *would say "Be more* ***positive****"*

Control your Thoughts

You are today where your thoughts have brought you. You will be tomorrow where your thoughts will take you.

One experiment was conducted by a primary school teacher upon their pupils, which shows how human beings move in the direction where their thoughts take them.

The teacher told the class that in a recent scientific study it has been discovered that the children who have blue eyes have greater natural ability to learn things faster than those with the brown one. Then she divided the class into two groups. One was the group with blue eyes children while the other was of the brown eyes students.

After a week or so, it was noticed that the students who had blue eyes shows a considerable progress than those who had brown ones and the progress of the students with brown eyes fell noticeably and measurably.

The next day teacher made a shocking announcement to the class that she had made a big, very big mistake. That she has told them exactly opposite of what the scientific study said.

She said, 'it was the students with blue eyes who were slower to learn and not the brown eyes one.' The children with the brown eyes are actually sharper, intelligent and faster to learn. Sorry for the mistake, children, really sorry 'she added.

When the teacher made this announcement the results started getting opposite. Now the students with brown eyes showed considerable progress while the grades of those with the blue eyes fell.

As you can see here that the success has nothing to do with that color of the eyes, but with the color of your thoughts. Success don't come by chance, neither by mistake and nor by luck, you have to pull it out of its den hold it firm. You have to guide your thoughts for the same

"No wind can ever be in the right direction for the directionless ship."

As Albert Camus wrote,

"Real generosity towards the future consists in giving all to what is present."

Yet, on most days, our minds are in ten different places at any one time. Rather than enjoying the walk to work, we wonder what the boss will say to us when we get to the office or what we will have for lunch or how our children will do at school today. Our minds are like scampering puppies or, as they say in the East, like unchained monkeys, rushing from place to place without any pause for peace.

A focus mind is the key to success. If you keep jumping here and there you can achieve nothing.Even the sun fails to burn thin paper when its light is spread all over, but when we concentrate it using a magnifying glass it holds the capacity even to put a hole in wood.

Working smarter, not harder:

1) Plan your work regularly.

2) Prioritize your needs and wants.

3) Organize your schedule.

4) Delegate (represent that work).

5) Plan your future plan.

Dream big, Aim High and Work Towards your Goals:

The future belongs to those who believe in the beauty of their dreams.Success occurs when your dreams become bigger than your excuses.

"If people are not laughing at your goals then your goals are too small"

-Azim Premji

Shoot for the stars and even if you fail you will land on the moon.

Yes, they do say that when you write down your goals something magical will happen, but goals are not something you just right at your desk, on the door of your locker, on the walls, or on the paper everywhere. What it actually means is that something magical will happen when you write your goals on the wall of your heart and the locker of your brain. That way you will be determined towards it.

Getting serious about goals gives you direction, makes you alert towards opportunities and prevents you from sailing unguided on the tides of your destiny.

*"Set Your **Goals** ridiculously high so that you fail above everyone else **success"***

-James Cameron

Whatever you do, do it with complete determination. Because

"When you determine to do something from the heart, the whole world conspires to make it happen"

Clarity in Our Thoughts results in Clearer Goals.

We should know what we want and what we want to achieve. This is a necessary step if you are serious about achieving success and give it some good time and thought. Don't be too optimistic nor be too pessimistic about your plan. I would advise you to write down your goals on paper and in checklist form. Put a cross or tick in front of them after regular intervals of time and never mark partially achieved goals.

*"If you can't **explain** it simply, it shows that you have not understood it **well** enough"*

-Einstein

Entrepreneurship:

*"If you don't **work for your dreams,** someone else will hire you to work for his own"*

To be an entrepreneur, you need to learn to-

Take risks and live them:

When we stop taking risks we actually stop living life because the boat is not made for the coast, it is made to be out in the sea and sail over the tides. The boat who ensures its safety by staying in the bay misses the fun and loses the fruits.

"Some failures in life are inevitable. It is impossible to live without failing at something unless you live so cautiously that you might as well have never lived at all. In which case you failed by default"

-J.K. Rowling

"In India, people are very afraid of failing. In the US, people fail and move on. Here you try to find out the ten reasons why you failed, everything except 'you'. In the US, failure is like a badge of honor. Oh, you have been to the war, you have been shot, and you must have been a good soldier! India has to develop that culture."

-Dr. Gururaj Deshpande, Co-founder, Sycamore Networks.

We have to be fearless to take risks and come out of our comfort zones and this is the only reason why there are more job seekers in India than job creators and why the economy is lacking behind and the exports are decreasing and the imports are hiking.

One must have a very stable amount of Self Confidence. No over confidence and no under Confidence because once we believe that Yes We can, We are half way there. We must remember Success is most often achieved by those who don't know that failure is inevitable.

*"**Entrepreneurship** is a **responsibility** rather than a profession"*

Experience is the teacher:

"Be brave take risks because nothing can substitute experience"

Give Respect Take Respect:

One must have a low profile, but a very high thinking. No matter the height a person has achieved, his feet must be there on the ground, one can learn the same from the tree, no matter how tall it grows its roots are always attached to the ground.

"Live simply so that others may simply live."

One thing, which we should not forget while following the above is, while respecting others, we should not let our self-respect down. But self-respect is something that is to be commanded and not demanded.

Passion:

"How does one ***become*** *a* ***butterfly****? You must want to fly so much that you are willing to give up being a caterpillar"*

My father once told me that the work is like walking with a plough tied to yourself while passion is walking a puppy.

A plough is a hard-core material which doesn't want to get moving to any place, you have no desire to move it either, but for the sake of your work you have to pull it. You have to muster your determination to pull it away. Work is something you don't want to do, but you are stuck up with it and are bound to complete.

On the other hand, have you ever taken a puppy out for a walk? You can barely control it! When you're inside the house, as soon as it hears you, it starts running in circles in anticipation. It gets excited. It starts clawing at the door trying to get out. As soon as you get outside, what happens? It tries to run up the street. It runs to the next tree. It practically **pulls you** behind it, and about all you can do is guide it in the general direction you want to go.

While you are having passion for something, you have to force yourself to stop doing it and get some rest. You have to force your hands and your mind which don't want to leave the work. And that is how magically passion works.

Expression of Emotion

Your intellect may be confused, but your emotions will never lie to you.

"Sometimes no words just a ***genuine*** *curve* **(smile)** *have its* ***beautiful*** *way to set things straight."*

Ask for what you want-

If you don't ask, the answer will always be No. learn to ask, learn to ask the proper way, once you get good at it, the answer will always be yes. A positive mind set a confident gesture surely help you achieve this.

Friendliness:

"Smile at people everywhere you go. Don't just give them one of those half-smirk/head nod things. Raise your eyebrows, show those teeth, and chuckle while you smile. Next time you're at the store, give a full-hearted smile to at least three complete strangers. You'll be amazed at what this does for them and for you."

-Dan Pearce, Single Dad Laughing

"A good motto is using ***friendliness*** *but not your friends"*

Be a Good Listener: (Learn to be Silent)

"A good listener not only gets popular everywhere, but after a while he gets to know something"

The more you keep silence, the more you can listen. Showing up the desperation and being reactive all the time don't help. Sometimes you have to learn to keep calm and you will be surprised that how much you failed to listen.

But at the end of the day, it's all about selective listening

*"**Listening** is not about understanding the words of the questions asked, but it is about **understanding** why was the question asked in the first place"*

To give you an example of selective listening, let me share with you a story I read about a medical doctor who was invited as a guest speaker to address a group of alcoholics. He wanted to make a demonstration that would be powerful enough to make people realize that alcohol was injurious to their health. He had two containers, one with pure distilled water and one with pure alcohol. He put an earthworm into the distilled water and it swam beautifully and came up to the top. He put another earthworm into the alcohol and it disintegrated in front of everyone's eyes. He wanted to prove that this was what alcohol did to the insides of our body. He asked the group what the moral of the story was and one person from behind said, "If you drink alcohol you won't have worms in your stomach." Was that the message?

Of course not. That was selective listening—we hear what we want to hear and not what is being said.

Here are a few practical tips to become better at the art of listening:

- If you are speaking and the person you are having a conversation with has not said anything within the past sixty seconds, there is a good chance you have lost her and it's time to stop talking so much.
- Resist the temptation to interrupt. Catch yourself just before you do so and pay more attention to the content of what the other person is saying to you.
- If appropriate (i.e., in a business setting), take notes. Few things more readily show the other person in a conversation that you genuinely wish to learn from what he/ she has to say than pulling out a notepad and making notes.
- After the other person makes her points, rather than immediately responding with your opinion, reflect on what you have just heard. Saying something such as, "Just to make sure I understand you, are you saying?" and doing so with complete sincerity will bring you much closer to the people you interact with everyday of your life.
- Listening helps you to develop a good understandingof the person.

"If I don't ***like*** *that* **man**. *I must get to know him better"*

- Abraham Lincoln

Dressing:

A proper dress opens many doors. It's a sign of self-respect. Clothing is transformative, dress everyday as if you are going to meet your worst enemy cause when you put on something really beautiful, you feel something, a confidence, and a smile. In some form or the other we are always playing a dress up.

Creativity and Innovation:

*"**Innovation** distinguishes between a **leader** and a follower"*

-Steve jobs

Think logically, but think out of the box:

"Here's to the crazy ones. The misfits. The rebels. The troublemakers. The round pegs in the square holes. The ones who see things differently. They're not fond of rules. And they have no respect for the status quo. You can quote them, disagree with them, glorify or vilify them. About the only thing you can't do is ignore them. Because they change things. They push the human race forward. And while some may see them as the crazy ones, we see genius. Because the people, who are crazy enough to think they can change the world, are the ones who do."

-Apple Inc.

*"A man without **creativity is** like **a bird** without wings"*

Honesty

*"To gain complete **honesty**, it **is important** to let go all your fears and defense **mechanism**"*

It's also about honesty with self as well as the people. Broken promises, untold stories, hidden lies, incomplete truths, fake condolences that's the world you and me we are surrounded by. There was a time when words were powerful enough that you don't need to think twice. There was a time when giving a word to someone meant it was fulfilled no matter what. It used to depict the dignity, but now people started treating them so lightly, we tell a friend that we will call him/her for lunch next week knowing well that we don't have time, we promise to call back when we know we are not, we treat ourselves with high level resolution promises every year and we gift ourselves dosages of unfulfilled promises at the end of the same year. We should stop falling prey to habit of doing the wrong thing which get fuelled up everytime we fail to do the right ones.

Mother Teresa said *"There should be less talk; a preaching point is not a meeting point. What do you do then, take a broom and clean someone's house that says enough"* Be a person of your words rather than being all talk and no action

Don't Wear a Mask:

One of your greatest protections against making bad choices is to not put on any mask of anonymity.

"We all wear masks, and the time comes when we cannot remove them without removing some of our own skin."

–André Berthiaume

There will be great pressure on each of you to act out of character—even to wear a mask—and become someone who doesn't really reflect who you are or who you want to be. No man, for any considerable period, can wear one face to himself and another to the multitude, without finally getting bewildered as to which may be the true."

"If you wear a mask long enough, you begin to forget what you are yourself beneath"

Self-integration:

Real integrity is doing the right thing, knowing that nobody's going to know whether you did it or not. Maintain integrity because nothing else is going to last.

"You can fool some man all the time or all the man sometime, but you can't fool all of them all the time"

Learn to Forgive:

There is one beautiful story

Write it on the sand

Two merchants were travelling along an inhospitable mountain-route which winds across lonely windswept hills of Persia. They were glad to be together and they got each other's back as they were very old friends. Each one was accompanied

by a retinue (followers) of servants and a caravan (convoy), which was carrying their merchandise.

As they were crossing a treacherous and narrow pass, one of them, a man called Najib, lost his footing and fell in the wild foaming river. The other merchant, known as Mussa, leaped in after him without hesitation and saved his friend from drowning.

The friends embraced each other with tears in their eyes. Then Najib called his most skilled slaves and ordered them to carve the following words on the huge black boulder that stood nearby.

'Wanderers! Know that they're in the wild and lonely spot, Mussa heroically saved the life of his friend Najib" The friends continued their journey again.

Now, after many years later, they both happen to travel through exactly the same route again. Reaching the very spot where one saved the life of the other they both sat down, lighted their campfire and started cooking their delicious food. Sitting under the beautiful sky crowded with stars, they started discussing something and didn't take long when they happened to argue over some issue. In argument Mussa struck Najib' s face and he fell down, on the very same spot where they embraced each other a long ago.

Najib got up and looked at his friend for a minute. He picked up a small twig lying their nearby and wrote the following words on the white sand near that huge black boulder (stone/ sarsen):

'Wanderers! Know you that in this wild and lonely place, Mussa after a rival argument broke the heart of his friend Najib!"

One of the Najib's slave asked him that, "Sir, you recorded your friend heroism on the rock, why is it that you write his cruelty on sand?"Najib replied 'I shall cherish the memory of my friend's kindnessand the brave assistance in my heart forever.

But the injured, he inflict onme, Ihope, will fade from my heart before these words fade from sand!" Forgive your friends-even before forgiveness is asked. And when you forgive –make sure you forget.

*"**Forgivenessis** that **sweet** fragrance the violet gives to the sandal that crushes it"*

Savour the Simple Stuff:

No one gets to take his possessions with him when he dies. I have yet to see a moving van following a hearse to a funeral. At the end of the day, the only thing we can take with us are our memories of all those great life experience that add meaning to our lives. Given this, I would rather spend my days doing things that will leave me happy memories than collecting possessions.

Dale Carnegie wrote, "*One of the most tragic things I know about human nature is that all of us tend to put off living. We are all dreaming of some magical rose garden over the horizon instead of enjoying the roses that are blooming outside our windows today.*" Have the wisdom to savor the simple things. The wonderful memories that they bring will add more value to your life than any of the material toys we spend so much life energy pursuing. As Emma Goldman noted, "*I'd rather have roses on my table than diamonds on my neck.*"

Time Management (Master your time):

'Time is not measured by the passing of years, but by what one does, what one feels, and what one achieves."

We procrastinate (postpone) and put the achievement of our dreams on hold while we tend to those daily emergencies that fill up our days. This is a certain recipe for a life of regret. As novelist Paul Bowles once wrote:

Because we don't know [when we will die], we get to think of life as an inexhaustible well. Yet everything happens only a certain number of times, and a very small number, really. How many more times will you remember a certain afternoon of your childhood, some afternoon that's so deeply a part of your being that you can't even conceive of your life without it? Perhaps four or five times more. Perhaps not even that. How many more times will you watch the full moon rise? Perhaps twenty. And yet it all seems limitless.

We tend to do anything for a little time but at the end, we regret for not having enough. Time and tide wait for none. As to sail over the tides, the sailor needs to master it, as the sailor of our own life we are bound to master the time. Once I happen to read a story,

An imaginary, but real bank account

Imagine you have a bank account which is credited with a fixed amount of money in the morning without fail. Suppose a thousand rupees. The only condition

that you need to take care of is that the amount can be used the same day and not the other day. Because In the evening, the balance whatever it is, not carried over to the next day, and your account balance becomes zero.

The next day your account will be credited back with thousand rupees once again with the same condition. Now it's up to you that whether you use it full, half or the complete amount, but remember the account balance will be zero the next day.

Not to worry the next day thousand rupees again. Should someone have such an account what would they think they will do? Isn't it amazing to know what will most people do?

Most people will want to use the maximum amount if not all because it won't be carried the next day.

Well, everybody has such an account. Though not of money, but of time. Every morning 24 hours are credited to our account. At the end of the day the balance will be zero. The next day balance will be zero. So why waste it, when we can use it to the full extent or at least maximum and it's free, it's with everyone. But we must remember one thing that though it's free, it's not inexpensive.Time is running. Make the most of it.

*"You can **delay** but time will **not**"*

Plan Your Work and Work your Plan:

*"The **plan** is nothing. Planning is **everything**" –Napoleon*

1) Set a goal.
2) Make plans.
3) Get to work.
4) Stick to it.
5) Reach goal.

"If I had eight hours to cut down a tree, I will spend six hours to sharpen my axe"

-Abraham Lincoln.

Being Proactive not Reactive:

"If you're proactive, you don't have to wait for ***circumstances*** *or other people to* ***create*** *perspective expanding* ***experiences****. You can consciously create your own."*

As per studies

- A reactive leader needs to have and use own answers while a proactive leader understand the power of team.
- A reactive leader is tellingoriented, but proactive leader is coaching oriented
- A reactive leader is concerned about self-first while proactive leader values the team first
- Reactive leader is afraid of control while proactive leader knows the best outcomes of giving up control
- Reactive leader uses rules to make decision and is quick to punish, while the other uses the principles and motivate to learn.

Steps to be a proactive leader.

- **Predict**: In order to be proactive, you must first develop foresight.
- **Prevent**: Proactive people see potential obstacles and exert their power to find ways to overcome them before those obstacles turn into concrete roadblocks.
- **Plan**: Proactive people plan for the future.
- **Participate**: Proactive people are not idle observers, they are active participants.
- **Perform**: Being proactive means taking timely, effective action.

Take Actions (Developyour Skills, Take Initiatives)

*"****Wisdom*** *is knowing what to do next, skill* ***is*** *knowing how to do it, and virtue is* ***doing*** *it,"-David Starr Jordan.*

Thinking big is one thing and yes it is important, but what is more important is to take action. The habit of just thinking and not doing at all is not going to take any of us anywhere. We people know what to do and how to do and even when to do, but we lack 'doing' once we achieve it no one can stop us from achieving even the impossible.

"To be on the Everest, you are not supposed to be ever at rest."

When you take initiatives you need to learn the art of decision making and working with team spirits

*"I don't **believe** in taking the right decisions, I believe **in** taking **the** decisions I like and then making them **right**"*

– Adolf Hitler

And what comes along with decisions are responsibilities. Learn to take responsibilities and not to blame any single person from the team.

Be a Leader:

A leader's job often includes changing your people's attitudes and behavior. Some suggestions to accomplish this:

- **Principle 1** - Begin with praise and honest appreciation.
- **Principle 2** - Call attention to people's mistakes indirectly.
- **Principle 3** - Talk about your own mistakes before criticizing the other person.
- **Principle 4** - Ask questions instead of giving direct orders.
- **Principle 5** - Let the other person save face.
- **Principle 6** - Praise the slightest improvement and praise every improvement. Be "hearty in your approbation and lavish in your praise."
- **Principle 7** - Give the other person a fine reputation to live up to.
- **Principle 8** - Use encouragement. Make the fault seem easy to correct.

- **Principle 9** - Make the other person happy about doing the thing you suggest.

(Source-Internet)

*"For the **strength** of the pack is the wolf and the strength of the wolf **is** the **Pack**."*

-Phil Jackson, Coach, Chicago Bulls.

Keep Your Cool:

*"Anybody can **become** angry — that is easy, but to be angry with the right person and to the right degree and at the right time and for the right purpose, and in the right way — that is not within **everybody's power** and is not easy."*

-Aristotle

Higher the post of a man gets the more cool he needs to be. You all may have observed that between the security guard and the CEO of a company, the CEO always have a better control over himself, he knows how to keep cool and how to be polite and that's what differentiate him from that rude security guard.

"We are not punished for our anger but by our anger"

– Gautam Buddha.

Communication Skills:

*"The art of **communication** is the language of **leadership**" because technical knowledge can get you a job, but communication skill can break us a manager*

Here are a few tips to improve your communication skills-

- Listen, notice the non-verbal cues and learn to get behind people's eyeballs.
- Always focus on the result.
- Don't let distractions affect you.

- Don't be shy to follow up and ask questions.
- Stay positive and show appreciation.
- Prepare a script if necessary.
- Tell a story,it creates interest and don't let the conversation suck.
- Get rid of Umm and Ahh, while talking, you could also try taking your hands out of your pockets or simply relaxing and pausing before you speak.
- Watch your body language and the tone of speaker and yourself.

Public Speaking-

"The success of your presentation will be judged not by the knowledge you send but by what the listener receives. "All you need is something to say, and a burning desire to say it. It doesn't matter where your hands are."

Observation:

Look wherever everyone looks, but see what no one else sees- the winner's way.

"Do stuff. Be clenched, curious. Not waiting for ***inspiration****'s shove or society's kiss on your forehead. Pay attention. It's all about* ***observation. Attention*** *is vitality. It connects you with others. It makes you eager. Stay eager."*

–Susan Sontag

Reading:

You know what ***books are*** *your* ***best*** *friends, they never hurt you, never leave you, and no complains no demands!!!*

Don't finish everything you start to read. It is so easy to feel compelled to finish every news, book you start. A great sense of guilt fills our minds if we do not reach the end of that book we used our hard – earned dollars to buy. But not every material deserves to be read in its entirety. As Fracis Bacon said, "Some books are to be tasted, others to be swallowed, and some few to be chewed and digested: that is, some books are to be read only in parts, others to be read, but not curiously, and some few books to be read wholly, and with diligence and attraction."

"One must know when to turn the page and when to close the chapter"

Go on a new fast.

I know so many people who begin their days by reading less than uplifting newspaper stories and who end them by catching up on the latest crimes, accidents and scandals on the late – night news.

Just do one thing daily, promise yourself that you will feed yourself with the positive news only as it not only develop a positive attitude, it also prevents the negative impact and negative thought on self. And you will notice that you haven't lost anything big, in fact, not at all, you get to know about all the news through general conversations and other such means, so it is always better to be selective about the things you read and news you go through.

Proficiency in Languages:

When you talk to people in the language they are comfortable with, the chances of getting you connected to them increases. Suppose you are in Maharashtra and you speak out few words in Marathi in your public appearances or in Local language with the Rickshwala you surely gets connected more easily. When Obama or a celebrity speaks *Namaste India*we all applaud. Because languages connect the people to people and heart to heart. It helps the others to get comfortable with you as well as they open up more. It develops a sense of belonging within them.

Have a Sense of Humour:

Humor Attracts people to you and you to the people. People like to laugh, they like to get rid of their stress and just have a good time. As a result, they tend to like hanging around with people who make them laugh and are fun to be with.

"In conversation, ***humor is*** *worth more than wit and easiness more than* ***knowledge****."*

– George Herbert

By having a sense of humor you can build your social circle and get to know more interesting people. (You may even find that more people flirt with you too, and are attracted to you because you are fun to be around)

It Attracts the Right Kinds of People

Attracting people into your life makes things more enjoyable, but it isn't about how many people you know, instead it is about the quality of the people that you know.Having a good sense of humor tends to attract others with a good sense of humor or with at least a positive outlook on life.

As you learn to have fun and to laugh about your challenges, you will find others who also bring in a positive vibe. These people can influence you in a good way. When you spend time with others who give off positive energy it helps you to stay positive in life and to always see the joy in the world.

Cope with Stress:

Stress is something we all have to deal with. The more you try to do, the more stress you will undoubtedly run into. The secret is not to let the stress, slow you down. Instead, keep moving in the direction you want to go and keep searching for solutions.

"A person without a sense of humor is like a wagon without springs. It's jolted by every pebble on the road.

– 'Henry Ward Beecher

While there are some great stress relieving activities, nothings gets rid of a stressful day like humour. Laughing helps you forget about your problems for a while so you can look at them with a clearer mind later on.

Health Benefits:

Laughing has been shown to improve your immune system by helping your body produce more infection fighting materials and lower the amount of stress hormones in your body.

Beside from that it has also been shown to relax your muscles and lower your blood pressure, making it a great way to keep your heart healthy and lower your chances of having a heart attack or stroke.

Improves Mood:

I'm sure I don't really need to tell you that laughing improves your mood and helps you feel better about yourself and life in general. Sometimes we need to stop focusing on the things which are stressing us out and start focusing on things which are making us feel good about the world in which we live.

Strengthen Friendship:

People feel closer to others who they are able to have a good laugh with. By joking around with friends and family you are not only enjoying a good time with someone you care about, you are also building a bond and a memory that you guys will be able to come back to later on.

Having an "inside joke" between your group can help to strengthen your relationship. And in some sense that is what life is all about.

Apply Break to your Worries

The Sanskrit character for funeral pyre is strikingly similar to the Sanskrit character for worry.

"One burns the ***dead*** *while the other burns the* ***living.****"*

Though we say that we are happier than our forefathers and we have less worries, our life is more comfortable and easier, but the truth is that we all have lost our abilities to smile. Stop worrying and start living.

Gift Yourself with '*Me* Time'.

The Sunday is kept at the end of week and it is a holiday that must be not a coincidence. There should be some reason behind it being a holiday. It is reserved for some of the most important, yet generally neglected tasks like time for family, some household works, and time with the loved ones. You need time for yourself. You strive hard the week long for everyone, but in this race you should not forget about you.

Your 'Me time' must be an inseparable part of your to do list, it doesn't matter what people think what you have to accomplish by it, but what matters is that you give yourself some space, it is not necessarily a week long, even a short nap in the Sunday afternoon, singing to your favorite song, relaxing under the open sky is worth it

Gratitude and Kindness: Gratitude is the Best Attitude

Story

Once there was an old man who asked some youngsters that what will they do suppose he gave them 1 million$. All the youngsters were surprised, some were in excitement and some were thinking what nonsense this man is talking. Some already started making plans about the use of money. Some said I will invest it. One said I will clear my debts and start a business. One said I will do charity. All of them replied with such big dreams. While one boy was standing silently, the old man asked him, "Son, what will you do?" he said "Sir, the first thing I will do is thank you to express my gratitude towards your kind deed" and the man presented him the money.

"I still have my feet on the ground, I just wear better shoes"

– Oprah Winfrey

The main thing to be learned from this incident is that, no matter what you get, when you get how much you get or how big you get, you must always remember from where it all came and your gratitude must be expressed without fail. Saying a little thank you is not a big deal at all, but it's not small either, it matters where you use it, the incident also teaches us that you should not be distracted from your ethics and values when you are rising high. The huge amount of money pulled all the others out of their path that they got so excited and desperate that they even couldn't think of saying a normal thank you to express gratitude.

"Kindness is simply the rent we pay for the space we use on this planet which gives us double the investment"

Be a Part of the Solution:

"If ***youare*** *not the part of* ***the solution*** *you are certainly the part of the problem"*

When you just give an eye to the problems and words for the solution and there is no way you are helping in solving the problem, you are of no use, you become the part of the problem and it takes no time when you yourself become the problem. A single helping hand is far better than a million praying lips they say, and they don't say it for no reason. Standing at the edge of the door with your hands fold doing nothing and just interrupting or giving advices makes you no hero.

We should take part in solving the problem, no matter, wecan't make a huge difference, butat least we don't come under the name of those who did nothing but under those who tried.

Patriotism:

Patriotism means to stand by the country. It does not mean to stand by the president or any other public official. It means-

- Special affection for one's own country.
- A sense of personal identification with the country.
- Special concern for the well-being of the country.
- Willingness to sacrifice to promote the country's good.

*"****Patriotism*** *is supporting your* ***country*** *all the time and your* ***government*** *when it deserves it."*

Care for the Temple:

Temple not necessarily the stone carved marble temple with idols in it, staying grounded in the church for hours, pouring oil on the Shani Dev-Indian mythology is not necessary, the temple is where you attain peace, it may be gym it may be library, it may be research lab, the body is itself the temple and the soul is itself the God. Taking care of it not only add life to your years, but years to your life. Those who don't have time for maintaining their temple in healthy way should take out time for their illness.

Respect the Nature

*'When you take the **nature** lightly, you **will** be **astonish**ed and you will be blown when it will take **you** lightly."*

Be the Creator of your Destiny:

'The most beautiful task one can ever undertake is the task of creating himself"

The story of Gods

Buddhists have a little story which relates to the principle of power.

After creating man, gods were worried about the safety of the principle of power. They were worried that by chance if man got hold of it, things would get very difficult for them.

God could never afford to let this happen. So they decided to conduct an urgent meeting. The question was where to hide the principle of power to keep it safe and away from man.

One god suggested that 'the best place to hide the power is on the top of the highest mountain'. Another god disagreed, he said,' sooner or later the man will reach there and we will be in trouble'. Another god suggested hiding it at the bottom of the deepest sea, but this was again rejected as the man can reach there also.

One wise god was listening to this when he said that that 'if hiding the principle power is your serious interest, why not put it inside man himself. Man would never think of looking there'.

Upon hearing this every god instinctively knew that this was the real solution. And the motion was carried.

The moral of the story that can be drawn is that there is everything you need to succeed and create an impact on the world, it is inside you only. Most people find it hard to accept. They like to think that problems in their lives are because of others or surrounding circumstances or the environment.

They forget that "*Wherever you are, where you will go, what you are and what you will become the only responsible person is YOU and no one else*"But what one likes to think has nothing to do with what it is. It doesn't matter what you like the truth will always be the truth.

When a good archer misses the mark, he turns and looks for the reason within himself. Your failure to shoot the target isn't the mistake of the target or the wind. So he can't just look around himself over the surrounding or the sky and blame the wind. He has to look inside, to improve his aim, to improve himself.

The fact is that we are the creator of our own destiny. We are what we are because of ourselves. And we will what we will only because of ourselves and no one else.

You don't have to go anywhere, there is no need to dig wells or climb mountains. There is no need to keep searching and investigate anywhere. What is needed is purely introspection and

There you are standing right in front of your success. The next step will be just the leap needed to be taken. And at the end of the day work hard pray hard and trust God:

"*Never be afraid to* ***trust*** *an unknown future to a known* ***God.***"

Become a Volunteer:

"*I wept because I had no shoes until I saw a man who had no feet.*"

It is so easy to magnify our problems and lose sight of the many blessings we all have to be so very grateful for. Giving the gift of your time by volunteering to serve those who have less than you is an excellent way to remind yourself on a regular basis of the abundance that exists in your life.

"I don't know what your destiny will be, but one thing I do know: The only ones among you who will be happy are those who have sought and found how to serve."- Albert Schweitzer

Anne Morrow Lindberg wrote, "One can never pay in gratitude; one can only pay 'in kind' somewhere else in life." Volunteering affords you the chance to help others and pay back the debt owed to those who have helped you.

*"When you were **born**, you cried and the whole world rejoiced. Live your life in such a way that when you die, the world cries and you **rejoice**."*

–Saint Kabir. Ancient Sanskrit saying.

Talk to Yourself, Your Best Friend:

Select a phrase according to what you need from life or what you want to become and train your mind to focus on it, repeat it daily. Repeat your mantras slowly. Let them flow in your life as breath in your body because the words that enlighten the soul are more precious than jewels.

Introspection:

*"We search for **happiness** everywhere, but we are like Tolstoy's fabled beggar who spent his life sitting on a pot of gold, under him the whole time. Your treasure—your perfection—**iswithinyou** already. But to claim it, you must leave the buy commotion of the mind and abandon the desires of the ego and enter into the silence of the heart."*

– Elizabeth Gilbert

We cannot understand the world unless and until we try to understand ourselves. After all the changes beginwith us.

SWOT Analysis:

SWOT Analysis is a useful technique for understanding your Strengths and Weaknesses, and for identifying both the Opportunities open to you and the Threats you face. It helps you to understand yourself better and makes you take a look at what is the truth and makes you believe it. It gives you a look of inside you so you can develop yourself seamlessly.

Strengths:

- What do you do better than anyone else?
- Which of your achievements are you most proud of?

What values do you believe in that others fail to exhibit?

Weaknesses:

- What could you improve?
- What should you avoid?

Again, consider this from an internal and external basis: Do other people seem to perceive weaknesses that you don't see? Are others doing better than you?It's best to be realistic now, and face any unpleasant truths as soon as possible.

Opportunities:

- What good opportunities can you spot?
- What interesting trends are you aware of?

A useful approach when looking at opportunities is to look at your strengths and ask yourself whether these open up any opportunities. Alternatively, look at your weaknesses and ask yourself whether you could open up opportunities by eliminating them.

Threats:

- Could any of your weaknesses lead to threats?
- What obstacles you currently face?

Performing this analysis will often provide key information – it can point out what needs to be done and put problems into consideration.

And Most Important Keep Smiling:

Your thoughts influence you, you become what you think. Then why not think big good and positive. Laughing at your problems, making yourself feel confident when you are depressed can in fact really help you feel better.

You can start to *"Fake it till you make it"*

In other words, you can pretend to be the kind of person you wish to be. By consistently acting as a highly enthusiastic person might or as a truly confident person would, you will eventually take on these personal attributes.

"Don't waste your time judging the wrongs and the right of your life, it is a roller coaster, just live it."

Some Paradoxical Commandments by Kent M. Keith

"People are illogical, unreasonable, and self-centered. Love them anyway.

If you do good, people will accuse you of selfish ulterior motives.

Do good anyway.

If you are successful, you will win false friends and true enemies.

Succeed anyway.

The good you do today will be forgotten tomorrow. Do good anyway.

Honesty and frankness make you vulnerable.

Be honest and frank anyway.

People favor underdogs but follow only top dogs. Fight for a few underdogs anyway.

What you spend years building may be destroyed overnight. Build anyway.

People really need help but may attack you if you do help them. Help people anyway.

Give the world the best you have and you'll get kicked in the teeth.

Give the world the best you have anyway."

I HAVE LEARNED

(This part contains one liners about the moments and experiences which one experiences daily or in some part of his life)

Love

1. I have learned that when I'm single I see happy couples and when I am in a relationship I see happy singles.
2. I have learned that sometimes it's about values you assign to things and not the promises you make.
3. I have learned that those two people who are meant to be together always find their way back they may lose their track, they may take time, they take few detours but they are never lost.
4. I have learned that you can live only two ways, either you love only one, or you care about no one.
5. I have learned that there is a reason why it is called as falling in love, because it's unintentional, selfless and it just happens.
6. I have learned that the one who truly love us will never leave us.
7. I have learned that your first love might not be your last, but that's okay.
8. I have learned that life without love is barely living
9. I have learned that love is when the guy stops thinking about sex and the girl starts thinking about it.
10. I have learned that a guy promising marriage to a girl is prince of dreams for girls and asshole for boys.

11. I have learned that sometimes you need to forget people, even those who you want the most, which makes it a hard nut to crack.
12. I have learned that sometimes the person you want the most, is the person you are best without.
13. I have learned that no matter how many options you have, you set your heart on someone you can never have
14. I have learned that it doesn't hurt the most when the people you love the most are gone or taken away, but when you realize that they never existed.
15. I have learned when someone stops caring you lose all your rights and abilities to either love or hurt them.
16. I have learned that a smiling face is the best revenge for those who took away your smile
17. I have learned that people sometimes move on so quickly while you are just waiting for them to come back.
18. I have learned that when you start losing importance in the eyes of the person you fighting for you try harder, the harder you try the more you lose your respect and importance.
19. I have learned that when striving hard to get a person back it is very difficult to draw a line between two states till when to care and when to move on.
20. I have learned that we never respect and love those who love us and those whom we love end up using us.
21. I have learned - That although the word "love" can have many different meanings, it loses value when overly used.
22. I have learned that before you fall in love, you need to pass a hard course military training of emotions.
23. I have learned that love should be made feel and expressed and anger should be told.
24. I have learned that there are many ways of falling and staying in love.

25. I have learned - That writing, as well as talking, can ease emotional pains.
26. I have learned - That two people can look at the exact same thing and see something totally different.
27. I have learned that you can keep going long after you thinkyou're lost somewhere.
28. I have learned that sometimes the people you love the most are taken away, change, forgotten soon.
29. I have learned that a man won't love a lady he can't respect.
30. I have learned that when someone doesn't love you the way you want to do means that they don't love you with all they have.
31. I have learned that you can't understand a person completely if you don't talk to them till 4am.
32. I have learned that no matter how much I care, some people just don't care back.
33. I have learned that sometimes when my friends fight, I'm forced to choose sides even when I don't want to, even after knowing that no matter who wins, and I will be the one who will lose.
34. I have learned when you are hurt the person you love the most and hate like hell is the same person.
35. I have learned that a boy and a girl can never be best friends because there comes a time whenever either one of them falls in love with the other and chances everything.
36. I have learned that when the love strikes us for the first time we are not perfect we make mistakes, we hurt and we get hurt, but when we learn to deal with ourselves most of the people don't dare to love again.
37. I have learned that sometimes it's the feeling or the relation that is more important than the person.

38. I have learned that one of the best feeling in life is when someone unexpected tells you about your likes and dislikes.
39. I have learned that there is a difference between loving someone and losing your self-respect to them.
40. I have learned that nobody is perfect until you fall in love with them.
41. I have learned that there comes a person in your life who makes you love the songs you never knew ever existed.

Happy Living

1. Looking back on the tears makes us laugh, but looking back on the laughs brings out the tear.
2. I have learned that all the fame and recognitions feels small when your dad tells his wife,how proud he feels about his son.
3. I have learned that sometimes to stop is as important as it to keep moving.
4. I have learned that the best thing of being happy without a reason is that neither it ends with the reason nor it requires one to occur.
5. I have learned that if everything will be beautiful then nothing will be beautiful.
6. I have learned that all those who hurt you in the past teach you that pain is not an excuse to quit the fight.
7. I have learned that forgiveness is the fragrance the violet gives the sandal that crushes it.
8. I have learned that *sympathy,* you get it from anybody, but jealousy, you have to earn it,
9. I have learned that if you think today is the worst day of your life, just relax, it certainly means that tomorrow is going to be better.
10. I have learned that sometimes spending money for the sake of spending money is worth spending money.

11. I have learned that you can't expect people to be nice to you because you are nice to them, because it's like expecting a dog not to bite you because you didn't bite him, but be nice anyway.
12. I have learned that the miracle is, the more you give, the more you receive, the less you get by sharing is fed back to you in the form of joy, happiness and satisfaction.
13. I have learned that it is always better to forgive others, not because they deserve forgiveness but because you deserve peace.
14. I have learned that you don't loseyourself, respect while fighting to get back the person who means something to you.
15. I have learned that caring is good, but like every other thing it has its limits.
16. I have learned that we don't have to change friends if we understand friends change.
17. I have learned that you can live a better life where no expectations are hurt when you start believing that everyone is good (Not always true).
18. I have learned *'Don't keep Expectations'* feels good to read in books and may make you feel strong and confident. It may make you worry less about yourself or you may feel like a hero. But it's not the case. You can't live without keeping expectations. They form the base and are automatically attached to the person you care and love and are proof of it.
19. I have learned that we all will miss the time when we can fit behind the dad's legs, certainly the best protection and the best place is your mom's lap.
20. I have learned that unless you don't learn to decide the priorities, your goodness and talent don't matter. Example: My mom learned to operate mobile phone and messaged me good morning, I didn't reply because it cost 1 rupee. Utter stupidity.

One should know where to apply which principles, where to save money and where not to.

21. I have learned that it's easy being good to someone, then being bad in a long run
22. I have learned that something you do in an instant can give you headache for life.
23. I have learned - That you shouldn't be so eager to find out a secret. It could change your life forever.
24. I have learned that it is better and easier to be good than being getting benefited by being bad because at the end of the day you neither have to confess to God nor you have to get worried of people's curse.
25. I have learned that no matter what happens, or how bad it seems today, life goes on, and it will be better tomorrow.
26. I have learned that life would have been better if god would have provided with background music.
27. I have learned that sometimes it doesn't matters to bunk the lectures if you don't miss the lessons.
28. I have learned that it is easy to imitate being good, but really a hard nut to crack when it comes imitating bad.
29. I have learned that many times you don't get what you desire for, but you get better.

Goals and Career

1. I have learned that while having any difficulty face it,don't lose heart, and be confident, you can solve it, don't cry you are not alone having difficulties.
2. I have learned that we are supposed to pursue what doesn't let us sleep.
3. I have learned that all you need is a job where you don't have to take a vacation from.

4. I have learned that we should be able to distinguish between what we like and what is right.
5. I have learned that spineless people will always turn on you.
6. I have learned that its success that can heal all the wounds that your heart or mind ever endeavored.
7. I have learned that there is a fine lap between letting it happen and making it happen.
8. I have learned that motivation once is not enough, did you stop bathing after having once.
9. I have learned that when you shed sweat in peace time, you don't have to shed blood in war times.
10. I have learned - That no matter the consequences, those who are honest with themselves get farther in life.
11. I have learned that Success is like the smell of shit, it can't be tolerated until it's yours
12. I have learned that you can keep going long after you think you are lost somewhere.
13. I have learned that achievement is not when you do something you are capable of, it's when you do something more than your capability.
14. I have learned that the very first time I failed was the time when I didn't trust myself that I can succeed.

•

"I have missed more than 9000 shots in my career. I have lost almost 300 games. Twenty six times I have been trusted to take the games, winning shot and I missed. I have failed over and over and over again in my life. And that is why I succeed."

-Michael Jordan

15. I have learned that when you don't grab the opportunities which knock your door, sooner or later the regret grabs you.

16. I've learned that the easiest thing is to fear and back out of the situation, but what I realized next is that the hardest part is living with the regret.
17. I have learned that when you do what you can, the god do what you can't.
18. I have learned that the best way to predict your future is to simply create it, as Einstein said don't worry about the future it comes soon enough.
19. I have learned that you need to take efforts to make things look effortless.

Yourself

1. I have learned that if there is nothing special in you, you are not special.
2. I have learned that we often keep searching for people who can change our lives, but always forget to look in the mirror.
3. I have learned that those people who doubt they are not good at anything are damn good at self-doubting.
4. I have learned that being stupid is like being death, you don't know about it but it's just hard for other people.
5. I have learned that I am constantly torn between 'I don't need anyone' and hey 'please fall in love with me'.
6. I have learned that once broken people are the strongest once they realize they can survive.
7. I have learned that constantly posting inspirational quotes on social networking sites is the first sign of depression.
8. I've learned that making a "living" is not the same thing as making a "life."
9. I've learned that whenever I decide something with an open heart, I usually make the right decision.
10. I have learned that sometimes it is better to know less, think less and be a fool.

11. I have learned that people know what your potential is. Better if even you know it.
12. I have learned that everyone in this world is self-centred, it's just the radius that matters.
13. I have learned - That the paradigm (pattern) we live in is not all that is offered to us.
14. I have learned that sometimes forgiving yourself matters more than being forgiven by others.
15. I have learned that maturity has much to do with the experiences you have and what you learn from them and not with the years you lived.
16. I have learned - That our background and circumstances may have influenced who we are, but we are responsible for who we become.
17. I've learned that even when I have pains, I don't have to be one.
18. I have learned that it's true you become what you choose and with whom you choose.
19. I have learned that when you are not a man of status and you disturb someone you love, neither she or nor anyone else going to like it, but when you have a status that is proved, the same action is considered to be great lovers.
20. I have learned that the hardest part is distinguishing and finding your way through what you know and what you don't want to believe.

Way of Living

1. I have learned that when you discuss more you lose the opportunity to learn more.
2. I have learned that the only way to progress is by drawing a bigger line and not rubbing the other ones.
3. I have learned that don't scare anyoneso much that he forgets to fear.

4. I have learned that power and money can corrupt you if you let it.
5. I have learned that there may be causes in world which are worth dying for but there is none worth killing for.
6. I have learned that for a pencil, a sharpener can the one cutting it short or the one making it sharp,
7. I have learned that sometimes it's better to take the stairs, because till the time one opens the door of the elevator, you reach your destination.
8. I have learned that don't dominate someone so much that he gets inspired.
9. I have learned that we all want to be different and that make us all the same.
10. I have learned that you can either exist between the limits or can live in the extremes.
11. I have learned that life is too small to commit your own mistakes, learn from others.
12. I have learned that sometimes no words just a genuine curve (smile) has its beautiful way to set things straight.
13. I have learned that the cause of many of the problems to grow and expand is the way they are condemned.
14. I have learned that corruption gives you piece of money, honesty gives you peace of mind.
15. I have learned that negative thinking isn't that bad when it got a right direction because it is the reason they invented the parachute.
16. I have learned that it is difficult to choose between being nice and getting hurt and having a sense of satisfaction and being bad and enjoy life by stepping on others.
17. I have learned that it's easy being good to someone, than being bad in a long run.

18. I have learned that it is better to remain silent and thought to be a fool than to speak and remove all doubts.
19. I have learned that it is important to be mature enough to understand where silence works better than the last word.
20. I have learned that no matter, we learned to use our tongue in 3 years but it takes a lifetime to know where to use it.
21. I have learned that when you keep saying 'You are not failed but your success is just postponed' then it makes you feel better in your eyes and fool in others. It is an excuse. Accept the truth. Embrace it. It will be your armour. Failing is learning.
22. I have learned that errors turning into mistakes if you keep yourself busy denying them.
23. I have learned that you shouldn't go through life with a catcher's mitt on both hands; you need to be able to throw something back.
24. I have learned that not a single piece of paper is meant to be wasted. If you put a plan on it, it can make you earn billions, if you print money on it you get a dollar, if you clean your shit it's a tissue.
25. I have learned that if someone treats you like a game, sometimes it becomes necessary to teach them how the game is played.
26. I have learned that confusing them when you can't convince them always works.
27. I have learned that when you think it can't go worse, it can and similarly when you think it couldn't have been better, it simply can.
28. I have learned that my birth was the only time when I cried and my mother smiled.
29. I have learned that one is lucky if he can cry, because later you can't even if you want to.

30. I have learned that a pile of shit can't feel proud just because flies are revolving around it.
31. I have learned that sometimes you know the answers, but not the questions.
32. I have learned that the belief which lies within drives the nature rather than the outer coverings.
33. I have learned that it is the time when you do something, your future self will be thankful for.
34. I have learned that all those who are drown or lost have to come back to the shore.
35. I have learned that life like it in the gangbanging way.
36. I have learned that people find it easier to forgive another for being wrong than being right.
37. I have learned that life is what happen to you when you are busy planning for something else.
38. I have learned that all those who wander are not lost.
39. I have learned that when you think things can't go better or worse, time has its miraculous ways of proving you wrong.
40. I have learned that sometimes memories (not forgetting anything) are a curse.

41. I have learned that life is governed by three simple laws-eat, pray, love.
42. I have learned that *karma* is like 69, you get what you give.
43. I have learned that no one wants to die, but everyone wants to go to heaven.
44. I have learned that happy are those to whom, when life gives lemons, they make lemonade. If you don't want lemonade, throw it back and say you wanted mangoes.
45. I have learned that there are three sides to an argument your side, their side and the right side

46. I have learned that some people are as useless as *'ay'* in *okay*.
47. I have learned that I always wonder how in a miraculous way money is the answer to all the questions these days.
48. I have learned that we all need help at times, but people respect those who help themselves and not the one who are always seeking.
49. I have learned that no matter who we are and what we are, we all have to wear those shoes once which you always tried to avoid.
50. I have learned that when you overuse something, it loses its capability to please you.
51. I have learned that nothing is more powerful than a truth whose time is now.
52. I have learned that making a "living" is not the same thing as making a "life."
53. I have learned that if you won't then, someone else will surely.
54. I have learned that twisted truths and repeating the lies don't make them real and true, but they don't even remain far different too.
55. I've learned that when you wish something life says yes and gives what you want, it says wait and gives you better and it says no and gives you the best.
56. I have learned that many times you don't get something not because you don't deserve it, but because you don't need it.
57. I have learned that we all have our happy moments and memories to celebrate, but the problem is that we don't cherish and are falling prey to sadness and jealousy seeing others celebrate their happy time.
58. I've learned that I don't mind when someone hurt me with even the bitterest truth. But I hate it most when someone comforts me with a lie.

59. I have learned that the best revenge you can take is by being happy.
60. I have learned that sometimes a *sorry* is better than a fight even when it's not your mistake.
61. I have learned that no one is independent in this world, we all are just interdependent.
62. I have learned that living up to just yourself can earn you nothing, while jolly people are always loved.
63. I have learned that if you give too much only in the first time then your graph falls down and so does your image.
64. I have learned that we cry when no one cares for us because we are busy ignoring those who care.
65. I have learned that it is not necessary to reply to all texts.

Social

1. I have learned that sometimes you have to put the individual ahead of their actions.
2. I have learned that society sees the results and not the efforts.
3. I have learned that the biggest problem with being punctual is that there is no onethere to appreciate it.
4. I have learned that if you give a person a mask, he will be his true self.
5. I have learned that it is cute to see how people are always there when they need you.
6. I have learned that not to judge people by their past, you will be unhappy when they put you there.
7. I have learned that success is relative, more the success more the relatives.
8. I have learned that you never get a second chance to make the first impression.
9. I have learned that just because someone rock, doesn'tmean that they are made up of stone.

10. I have learned that a girl born beauty is half married.
11. I have learned that when you get angry at someone easily who is better than you at something for his mistake and try to expose him to other people, it shows you are jealous.
12. I have learned that even when you think you have no more to give, when a friend cries out to you, you will find strength to help.
13. I have learned that some people are like crayon, they may not be your favourite one, but you will need them someday to complete your picture.
14. I have learned that sometimes the people you expect to kick you when you are down are the one who provide their shoulder to raise you high.
15. I have learned that when you lose hope, you come across some people in life who are like objects in the mirror, 'They are closer than they appear'
16. I have learned that mind your language, count your words, and mean what you say because otherwise people no longer stay.
17. I have learned that it's hard to determine, where to draw the line between being nice and not hurting people's feelings and standing up for what you believe.
18. I have learned that some people deserve a pat on the head with a hammer.
19. I have learned that when you try to impress too many people at a time and try to be good to everyone at once, you certainly end up being a villain in everyone's view.
20. I have learned that no matter how you try to protect your children, they will eventually get hurt and will hurt you in the process.
21. I have learned - That no matter how many friends you have, you will feel lonely and lost at the times you need them most.

22. I have learned that when you lend someone 1000 bucks and never see them again, then it's worth those 1000 bucks.
23. I have learned that your life can be changed in a matter of hours by people who don't even know you.
24. I've learned that regardless of your relationship with your parents, you'll miss them when they're gone from your life.
25. I have learned that everyday you should reach out and touch someone. People love a warm hug, or just a friendly pat on the back.
26. I have learned that people will forget what you said, people will forget what you did, but people will never forget how you made them feel.
27. I have learned that when you are weak without your family and you need them like nothing. It doesn't mean that you are weak, because one needs to be strong to admit it.
28. I have learned that a hug is the cheapest yet most valuable gift.
29. We all have to go through those situations which we once saw or made someone saw.
30. I have learned that when you are fighting with your brother, no matters who wins, it's always the mother who loses.
31. I have learned that everyone in this world is going to hurt you today or tomorrow, but at the end, it's us who have to decide what's important, the pain or the person.
32. I have learned that you can tell a lot about a person by the way he/ she handles these three things: a rainy day, lost luggage, and tangled Christmas tree lights.

At the end

I've learned that I still have a lot to learn.

A Random Story.

The Story of a Boy

"It's a skill, thought to be a fool and teach everyone a School."

A young boy enters a barber shop and the barber whispers to his customer, "This is the dumbest kid in the world. Watch while I prove it to you." The barber puts a dollar bill in one hand and two quarters in the other, then calls the boy over and asks, "Which do you want, son?" The boy takes the quarters and leaves. "What did I tell you?" said the barber. "That kid never learns!" Later, when the customer leaves, he sees the same young boy coming out of the ice cream store." Hey, son! May I ask you a question? Why did you take the quarters instead of the dollar bill?" The boy licked his cone and replied, "Because the day I take the

Dollar, the game is over!"

Hush!! Finally, you have successfully completed the book

That shouldn't be boring, I hope.

I wish you have taken at least something from the book. And no worries even if you haven't.

Whenever you need something, encouragement, courage guidance just bring this book out of your bookshelf, move your hand over the cover page and read out.I am sure you will always find something to your rescue

Just one last mail I want to share my dad forwarded me.

Written by Regina Brett, 90 years old, of the Plain Dealer, Cleveland, Ohio

My odometer rolled over to 90 in August, so here is the column once more:

1. Life isn't fair, but it's still good.
2. When in doubt, just take the next small step.
3. Life is too short – enjoy it.
4. Your job won't take care of you when you are sick. Your friends and family will.
5. Pay off your credit cards every month.
6. You don't have to win every argument. Stay true to yourself.
7. Cry with someone. It's more healing than crying alone.
8. It's OK to get angry with God. He can take it.
9. Save for retirement starting with your first pay check.
10. When it comes to chocolate, resistance is futile.
11. Make peace with your past so it won't screw up the present.
12. It's OK to let your children see you cry.
13. Don't compare your life to others. You have no idea what their journey is all about.
14. If a relationship has to be a secret, you shouldn't be in it.
15. Everything can change in the blink of an eye, but don't worry, God never blinks.
16. Take a deep breath. It calms the mind.
17. Get rid of anything that isn't useful. Clutter weighs you down in many ways.
18. Whatever doesn't kill you really does make you stronger.
19. It's never too late to be happy. But it's all up to you and no one else.

20. When it comes to going after what you love in life, don't take no for an answer.
21. Burn the candles, use the nice sheets, and wear the fancy clothes. Don't save it for a special occasion. Today is special. Yesterday was history, Tomorrow is Mystery but today is gift, that's why it is called as *present.*As said in Hindi- yesterday is called as *Bhoot kaal*-it contains *Bhoot*i.e. Demon tomorrow is called as *Bhavishya kaal*, it contains *Vishi* i.e. poison and today is called as *VartmaanKaal*, which contains *Maan* i.e. Pride.

"What if one day you wake up and realize that all your powers are lost, what will you do? Then I should make the most of today"

-Turbo-the movie

22. Over prepare, then go with the flow.
23. Be eccentric now. Don't wait for old age to wear purple.
24. The most important sex organ is the brain.
25. No one is in charge of your happiness but you.
26. Frame every so-called disaster with these words 'In five years, will this matter?'
27. Always choose life.
28. Forgive.
29. What other people think of you is none of your business.
30. Time heals almost everything. Give time time time.
31. However good or bad a situation is, it will change.
32. Don't take yourself so seriously. No one else does.
33. Believe in miracles.
34. God loves you because of who God is, not because of anything you did or didn't do.
35. Don't audit life. Show up and make the most of it now.

36. Growing old beats the alternative of dying young.
37. Your children get only one childhood.
38. All that truly matters in the end is that you loved.
39. Get outside everyday. Miracles are waiting everywhere.
40. If we all through our problems in a pile and saw everyone else's, we'd grab ours back.
41. Envy is a waste of time. Accept what you already have, not what you need.
42. The best is yet to come.
43. No matter how you feel, get up, dress up and show up.
44. Yield.
45. Life isn't tied with a bow, but it's still a gift."
46. If you think today is the worst day of your life, then why to worry? It means tomorrow going to be better.

Whichever age you are in

Dis age is never going to come back.....

So fall in love,

If you can't, have a new crush everyday.....

Dream...Imagine...

B impulsive...Go crazy......

Flirt...Get your heart broken...

Bunk d lectures....

Dance madly...

Click crazy...

Talk constantly...Laugh loudly...

Speak abusing words... Sing fav song...

Shout...Wander late night...

Take chances... Break d rules....

Make your own philosophy...

Smile & make others smile...

Go 4 it...Feel it...

Get over with it...

Live dis age!!

Coz things are going to be difficult n difficult tomorrow....

Remember not to make it complicated, the simpler the better. There are some people who like it another way round. They believe that

Big problems like "Where to land my private jet?" are always better than "When will I get my own home?"

The choice is yours!!

HANDY TIPS

From - Life's little instruction book.

The Basics

- *Take chances.*
- *Sing in the shower.*
- *Treat everyone you meet like the way you want them to treat you.*
- *Watch a sunrise at least a year.*
- *Never refuse homemade sweets.*
- *Strive for excellence, not perfection.*
- *Learn three clean jokes.*
- *Don't carry a grudge.*
- *Leave behind the orthodox approach.*
- *Sleep less.*
- *Stop thinking tiny thoughts.*
- *Don't worry about the things you can't change.*
- *Learn to meditate.*
- *Be an adventurer.*
- *Respect your instinct.*
- *Love your work.*
- *Have a family mealtime.*
- *Connect with nature.*

- *Take a mini vacation.*
- *Take a power nap at noon.*
- *See your days as your life.*
- *Don't be so hard on yourself.*
- *Remember recreation must involve re-creation.*
- *Choose worthy opponents.*
- *Find your places of peace.*
- *Don't waste time learning the tricks of the trade, instead learn the trade.*
- *Collect quotes that inspires you.*
- *Stop blaming others and start living.*
- *Be a good loser.*
- *Be a good winner.*
- *Determine what's right and not who is right.*
- *Think twice before burdening a friend with a secret.*
- *Praise in public.*
- *Criticize in private.*
- *Don't major in minor things.*
- *Don't tell anyone that they look tired.*
- *To win the war be prepared to lose some battles.*
- *Never cut what can be untied.*
- *Try for the best, prepare for the worst.*
- *Learn to show enthusiasm even you don't feel like it.*
- *Beware of the person who has nothing to lose.*
- *Everyday, show your family how much you love them. With your words, touch and thoughtfulness.*
- *Remember the overnight success have the work of 15 years behind it.*
- *Cut out newspaper article.*
- *Drink fresh fruit juice.*

- *Take a public speaking course.*
- *Rewrite your life story.*
- *Walk in the woods.*
- *Create a healthy environment.*
- *Listen to calm music.*
- *Be more than your moods.*
- *Create a daily code of conduct.*
- *Never overestimate your power to change others.*
- *Promise big, deliver big.*
- *Don't burn bridges; you will wonder how many times you have to cross the same river.*
- *Don't believe people when they ask you to be honest with them.*
- *When tempted to criticize, bite your tongue.*
- *Never underestimate power of love and forgiveness.*
- *Don't bore people with your problems. When someone asks you how you feel?Say terrific and when they ask you how is your work? Say excellent.*
- *Learn to disagree without being disagreeable.*
- *Be tactful. Never alienate anyone on purpose.*
- *Don't say you don't have enough time. You have same number of hours per day as Helen Keller, Jawaharlal Nehru, Einstein, Newton, Lincoln have.*
- *Live your life as an exclamation, not explanation.*
- *Instead of word problem replace it with opportunity.*
- *Give people the benefit of doubt.*
- *Always carry stamps in your wallet. You never know when you will find a perfect card for your loved ones.*
- *Be enthusiastic about the success of others.*
- *Return borrowed vehicles with petrol tank full.*
- *Leave everything a little better than you found them.*
- *Become the most positive and enthusiastic person you know.*

- *Say thank you a lot.*
- *Say please a lot.*
- *Avoid negative people.*
- *Wear polished shoes.*
- *Remember the special days.*
- *Have a firm handshake.*
- *Send a lot of valentine cards and have them signed.*
- *Look into the people's eyes.*
- *Be the first to say hello.*
- *Give your priorities straight. No one ever said on his death bed, 'I had only spent more time at the office.*
- *Return all things you borrow.*
- *Keep secrets.*
- *Plant flowers every spring.*
- *Always accept an outstretched hand.*
- *Wave at kids in the school bus.*
- *Don't be afraid to say 'I made a mistake'.*
- *Don't be afraid to say 'I don't know'.*
- *Marry only for love.*
- *Call your parents when you are away.*
- *When nothing goes right go to sleep.*
- *Tell the truth.*
- *Date someone totally wrong for you.*
- *Learn to say No.*
- *Gaze at the stars.*
- *Laugh like an idiot.*
- *Dance your heart out.*
- *Go to beach.*

- *Eat Ice Cream in rainy season.*
- *Feel the warmth and fuzzy about the one you love.*
- *Call someone late night.*
- *Bunk the daily routine.*
- *Lie on the grass and stare the sky.*
- *Listen to the radio.*
- *Watch the sunrise.*
- *Sing in bathroom.*
- *Spend all your money.*
- *Fall in love.*
- *Get to know someone random.*
- *Say I love you to someone in life and prove it.*
- *Be mean.*
- *Make fun of people.*
- *Sing out loud.*
- *Laugh at stupid joke.*
- *Cry.*
- *Take revenge.*
- *Surprise loved ones with unexpected gifts.*
- *Apologize.*
- *Laugh when you fall.*
- *Get into a fight.*
- *Tell someone how much they mean to you.*
- *Tell the idiot how he or she has hurt you.*
- *Tell someone what they are missing.*
- *Abuse.*
- *Sit alone, watch the rain and cry.*
- *Laugh till your stomach hurts.*

- *Pose stupidly for pictures.*
- *Give some1 a hug when they need it, make sure you get one when you do.*
- *Act like a kid.*
- *Be brave. Even if you are not, pretend to be. No one can tell the difference.*
- *Demand excellence and be willing to pay for it.*
- *Always remember the anniversaries.*
- *Preserve those special moments only for your spouse.*
- *Whistle.*
- *In business and in family relationships remember that the most important thing is trust.*
- *Never encourage anyone to become a lawyer.*
- *Never invest money in stock market more than you can afford to lose.*
- *Attend school reunions.*
- *Lend only those books you never care to see again.*
- *Always have something beautiful in sight may be as simple as rose in your garden.*
- *Think big thoughts, but live the small pleasures.*
- *Never cheat.*
- *Learn to identify local flowers, trees and birds.*
- *Consider writing a living will.*
- *Learn to listen. Opportunities sometimes knock very softly.*
- *Learn to tie a tie.*
- *Remember people's names.*
- *When starting out, don't worry about not having enough money. Limited funds are a blessing, not a curse. They encourage creative thinking.*
- *When someone is relating an important event in their life, don't try to stop them with a story of your own. Let them own the stage.*
- *Learn a foreign language.*

- *Keep your watch five minutes fast.*
- *Never deprive someone of hope. It might be all they have.*
- *Give yourself an hour to cool off before replying to someone who has provoked you. If it involves something really important then give 24 hours.*
- *Smell roses.*
- *Strive for excellence, not perfection.*
- *Make a will and tell your next of kin (blood relation) where it is.*
- *Don't waste time responding to your critics.*
- *Resist people telling how something should be done, instead tell them what needs to be done.*
- *Never give up on what you really want to do.*
- *Be kinder than necessary.*
- *Wear out, don't rust out.*
- *Never take actions when you are angry.*
- *Learn to recognize the inconsequential, then ignore it*
- *Be your love's best friend.*
- *Battle against prejudice (bias).*
- *Be romantic.*
- *Let people know what you stand for, and what you don't stand for.*
- *Ask why a lot.*
- *Measure people by the size of their heart, not the bank account.*
- *Go completely unplanned for a trip.*
- *Click lot of photos.*
- *Confess to God.*
- *See people walking in a park.*
- *Put your head in mom's lap.*
- *Don't be afraid to say I love you. Don't be strong enough to break their hearts.*

- *Meet shit ton of new people.*
- *Have a sense of humor.*
- *Travel alone with headphones on and let your mind think.*
- *Be nice to some stranger.*
- *Plant a tree you will never see again.*
- *Read your old books.*
- *Live fully so you can die happy.*